THE DECLARATION OF INDEPENDENCE AND GOD

"Self-evident-truths" was a profound phrase used by the drafters of the American Declaration of Independence to insist on their rights and freedom from oppressive government. How did this Enlightenment concept of self-evident human rights come to be used in this historic document, and what is its true meaning?

In *The Declaration of Independence and God*, Owen Anderson traces the concept of a self-evident creator through America's legal history. Starting from the Declaration of Independence, Anderson considers both challenges to belief in God from thinkers like Thomas Paine and American Darwinists as well as modifications to the concept of God by theologians like Charles Finney and Paul Tillich. Combining history, philosophy, and law in a unique focus, this book opens exciting new avenues for the study of America's legal history.

Owen Anderson is an associate professor of philosophy and religious studies at Arizona State University. His books include *Reason and Faith in the Theology of Charles Hodge* (2014), *Reason and Faith at Early Princeton* (2014), *The Natural Moral Law: The Good After Modernity* (2013) and *The Clarity of God's Existence* (2008), which study the ethics of belief in God, how God can be known, and the knowledge of God as the highest good.

The Declaration of Independence and God

SELF-EVIDENT TRUTHS IN AMERICAN LAW

Owen Anderson
Arizona State University

CAMBRIDGE
UNIVERSITY PRESS

CAMBRIDGE
UNIVERSITY PRESS

32 Avenue of the Americas, New York, NY 10013-2473, USA

Cambridge University Press is part of the University of Cambridge.

It furthers the University's mission by disseminating knowledge in the pursuit of education, learning, and research at the highest international levels of excellence.

www.cambridge.org
Information on this title: www.cambridge.org/9781107088184

First published 2015

A catalog record for this publication is available from the British Library.

Library of Congress Cataloging in Publication Data
Anderson, Owen J., author.
The Declaration of Independence and God : self-evident truths in American law / Owen Anderson, Arizona State University.
pages cm
Includes bibliographical references and index.
ISBN 978-1-107-08818-4 (hardback)
1. Religion and law – United States. 2. United States. Declaration of Independence I. Title.
KF358.A53 2015
340′.11–dc23 2015016105

ISBN 978-1-107-08818-4 Hardback

To John and Leanna

CONTENTS

Preface *page* ix

Introduction: The Formula of the Declaration of Independence: Epistemology, Metaphysics, Ethics 1

1 Thomas Jefferson and Thomas Paine. 31

2 The Reformed Influence on Common Sense Philosophy 50

3 Common Sense and the Self-Evident in Law 69

4 Intuition and the Self-Evident in Law 86

5 Naturalism, Darwinism, the Self-Evident, and Law. . . . 100

6 Revivalism, New Religious Movements, and Law 124

7 Liberal Theology and Legal Transformations 140

8 Secular and Religious Goods in the Twentieth Century. . 157

Conclusion: Building on Past Insights: A Philosophy of History 173

Notes 179

Bibliography 191

Index 197

PREFACE

This book is the product of my time as a research fellow in the James Madison Program at Princeton University. There I was able to pursue the question of what the Declaration of Independence means when it says that it is self-evident that God created humans. This book is a continuation of the research in my previous books. Wanting to know what is the highest good motivates these books. Early in my studies of philosophy, I came to recognize the difference between having an opinion, even a true opinion, and having knowledge. The many attempts to explain the diference between knowledge and opinion often by-pass the role of reason in showing what is clear. In topics such as *God* and *the good*, there are many competing beliefs or opinions. If we are responsible for knowing what is good then it must be clear to reason what is good.

I also came to understand that if we cannot know what is good, then we cannot be held responsible for failing to pursue the good. If we cannot know what is good, then it is a mere accident whether a person is pursuing what is actually good. This same is true about knowing God. If God cannot be known, then we cannot be held responsible for failing to know God. Out of this understanding came my desire to study our ability to know the good and God and contrast this with skepticism and fideism about these subjects.

This book was inspired by my children. They remind me that we are born asking fundamental philosophical questions. From our earliest years, we ask the basic questions about knowledge, reality, and the good. My hope for myself, for them, for my students, and for my readers is that we will continue to pursue this knowledge about the highest good.

INTRODUCTION: THE FORMULA OF THE DECLARATION OF INDEPENDENCE

Epistemology, Metaphysics, Ethics

> "They say they want the kingdom
> But they don't want God in it."[1]

The Declaration of Independence serves the role of a creed in American thought and history. It was framed after a century and a half of colonial history. Although attributed to Thomas Jefferson, its final form included edits by a committee, and delegates from the colonies signed it. The largest part of its body is a list of grievances against the king, and it describes itself as a defense of the separation between England and the colonies. However, in giving this defense, it gives a succinct foundation of the epistemology, metaphysics, and ethics on which the defense rests. These three areas form the foundation of a worldview about knowledge, God and man, and the pursuit of the good life. This foundation is stated in the well-known phrase "We hold these truths to be self-evident, that all men are created equal, that they are endowed by their Creator with certain unalienable Rights, that among these are Life, Liberty, and the pursuit of Happiness." The Declaration of Independence serves to give the beginning ideas for the country. Part of this study is to understand what role God the Creator plays in that country and what role God plays in the kingdom.

BASIC BELIEFS

Before getting into the historical analysis, we need to set the context by doing work in philosophical prolegomena. Since this study includes the idea of self-evidence, we need to get into focus related ideas about reason, belief formation, and the laws that govern belief formation. The sections that follow provide a look at these topics. We will be studying the most basic questions that humans can ask. Epistemology is the theory of knowledge. It asks what is knowledge and how it is different from correct opinion. How can we be certain in our beliefs rather than possibly mistaken? The source of knowledge is the source of authority. Authorities are cited to justify knowledge claims, and the highest authority cannot be questioned because it makes questioning possible. The Declaration of Independence claims that there are some beliefs that are self-evident. For something to be self-evident means that its truth is evident to a person once its meaning is understood. This is different than most beliefs, which, even when their meaning is understood, require support from other beliefs to demonstrate their truth. A distinction might be made between what is self-evident and what is self-attesting. To be self-attesting means the belief proves itself. It cannot be false without violating the very laws that define thought. To be self-evident is a more subjective claim. A statement might appear self-evident to one person and not self-evident to another. Whether a statement is self-attesting can be objectively determined by understanding the laws of thought. The subjective nature of *self-evident* has reverberated in American history.

Metaphysics is the study of what is real. There is a difference between what is real and what only appears to be real. There is also a difference between what is temporary and what is permanent or eternal. Something can be real now but not real in the past or in the future. What is eternal has always been real; what is eternal had no beginning and, therefore, will have no end. The Declaration of Independence sums up its claims about what is real by affirming that humans are created by God. In making this statement, it affirms that some things – God – are eternal and other things – the creation, including humans – had a beginning. Beyond this, it does not define *God*. This has left open an ambiguity that has developed into great divisions within American thought and life.

Ethics is the study of what is good. It distinguishes between means and ends. Although there are many proximate ends, the final or highest end is that toward which all choice aims. The good is distinct from the duties, virtues, and obligations required to achieve the final end. It is also distinct from happiness, which is an effect of achieving what one believes to be good. Because a person can be mistaken about what is actually good, there is a difference between happiness and lasting happiness. Lasting happiness is only possible if what is actually good has been attained. The Declaration of Independence forms its ethical theory around a theory of rights. Humans are said to have a right to their life and the freedom to pursue what they believe will make them happy. This tells us about the limits of government in human life. However, it does not make a statement about what is actually good or about what will bring lasting happiness. Ever since the Founding there have been internal and external struggles over how to understand the good.

In the following, we will consider the relationship between knowing what is real and the good. It is formally true that the highest good is knowledge of the highest reality. However, competing worldviews understand the highest reality differently. Here we will see competing definitions of "God," as well as philosophical materialism, which states that only the material world is real, and pantheism, which says that all being is God. This means that what is at stake in navigating these competing claims about reality is the highest good itself. This is both intensely personal for each of us and incredibly important for a society. It is the highest good that gives meaning to life and provides unity and direction for society. If the highest good is not known, then meaning and unity are lost. Where there are competing beliefs about the good, then there will be division that prevents growth and ultimately undermines culture. Therefore, I am proceeding with the belief that the study of the good and consequently the study of knowing God is basic and must be in place if other important matters are to be known and divisions to be settled.

There can be no more important subject to set in place than good and evil. Plato discusses the good in book 7 of *The Republic*. Aristotle's *Nicomachean Ethics* makes it the original and central question. It is not a new question for humans or in philosophy. It is a foundational question. As the founder of the Academy, Plato made it a subject that continues down in the Academy to this day. Getting the good in place is a central issue for each of us in our individual lives, in the Academy as it proposes to benefit human society and search for knowledge, and in society as it works together to pursue and increase what is good for all.

CREEDS AND THE AMERICAN REVOLUTION

It is important for any creed to establish its beliefs in the three areas of epistemology, metaphysics, and ethics. It is also important for a creed to be succinct and direct so as to be widely understandable. However, when *succinct* is replaced with *ambiguous*, the outcome will be disagreement and division. The following is a study of how these central ideas in the American creed have been diversely understood, the challenges that have been raised by competing understandings, and the ways that unanswered and remaining challenges continue to divide Americans over knowledge, what is real, and what is good. Understanding these ideas helps us unlock the flow of American history.

A creed is an attempt to express as consciously and consistently as possible the foundational beliefs of a group. Creeds reveal the extent to which the writers are conscious of what is foundational. The foundational questions are the most basic that can be asked. They involve those just discussed about knowledge and authority, the eternal and what is real, and the good and lasting value. They also reveal the extent to which the writers are conscious of what is necessary in giving a coherent and true answer to foundational questions. A creed attempts to give a system or consistent set of beliefs. In this sense, a creed is the most conscious and consistent formulation of a foundation that the writers can give.

The American Revolution is not the beginning of American history. It is a product of patterns of thought dating to the start of the English colonies. Although the American Revolution is said to have occurred within a generation that took a more secular turn than any of its predecessors, it still relied on categories of thought and a dialectic that had been working itself out through events like the First Great Awakening. These include dichotomies that continue to form the essence of divisions in America: tradition versus individual experience; individual and collective duty versus pleasure and happiness; worldly goods versus heaven; liberty versus license. Accordingly, the American Revolution has been interpreted in competing ways: there is an economic interpretation, a political interpretation, a "spirit of the people" interpretation, and others. Each of these focuses on what is undoubtedly an aspect of the events. In order to unite them, we must bring into focus the most basic beliefs that animated the revolution. These are beliefs about knowledge, what is real, and what is good. These basic beliefs help explain why a given economic or political theory was taken and are at the heart of understanding the spirit of a people.

Changes in basic beliefs over time explain changes in the country. History studies change, and it is understanding the changes in basic beliefs that helps unite understanding the changes in other areas of human life. A basic belief is a belief that is presupposed by another belief. The most basic beliefs are those beliefs that are presupposed by all other beliefs in a belief system or worldview. Humans are never totally conscious or completely consistent, so it might be tempting to say that humans do not have worldviews. However, as challenges arise to a person's or group's belief, this forces greater consciousness and consistency in expressing the meaning of beliefs and how they relate to each other. The alternative is to say that all beliefs are equally true or can be held with any other belief so that in the end, it doesn't really matter what you believe. This is a form of nihilism.

This process of challenges to basic beliefs will help us understand the changes in American thought. People rely on their basic beliefs to give meaning to their lives. When a basic belief is challenged as false or meaningless, this threatens the meaning of life. This threat cannot go unanswered because it is a threat to everything else a person understands. Of the various needs, the need for meaning is basic. Although people may say they find meaning in how they feel or in what they choose to do, behind feelings and actions are beliefs. Even the statement that I find meaning in my feelings is a belief. The role of beliefs in interpreting experiences for meaning is unavoidable. That beliefs are ordered from more to less basic is also unavoidable. Therefore, in order to understand how people find meaning and how meaning is actually to be found, we must look at basic beliefs and critically analyze them for coherence.

MEANING AND REASON

In order to make progress in our thinking about the self-evident, we will need to also take time to think about reason, meaning, and the relationship between beliefs from basic to less basic. Meaning can have different meanings. To say something is meaningful can be to say it has purpose. Or it can be rich in significance. However, both of these presuppose the kind of meaning that a belief has. A belief, expressed in a sentence or judgment, combines concepts to affirm or deny something about them. It is meaningful insofar as it has not put these concepts together in a way that is contradictory. Meaning is had when the laws of thought are used. These have classically been called *reason* and refer to the laws of identity (*a* is *a*), excluded middle (either *a* or *non-a*), and noncontradiction (not both *a* and *non-a*). Concepts are formed when we distinguish *a* from *non-a*. Judgments are made when we relate concepts to each other. Arguments are made when judgments are used to support a conclusion. Reason cannot be questioned or doubted since it is by the laws of thought that questions and doubts are formed. It would be a category mistake to ask "how do we know the laws of thought are true?"

The point of taking the time to define *reason* and *meaning* is that both of these terms play a role in how basic beliefs are formed and used to interpret experience and what it means for something to be self-evident. It is also because both of these terms are a part of the unfolding challenges to the foundation expressed in the Declaration of Independence. We will see competing ideas about how *reason* is defined and conflicting accounts of what is *meaningful*. In each of these, the formative meaning of *reason* as the laws of thought used to form concepts, judgments, and arguments will be found throughout. Similarly, the critical use of reason as the application of the laws of thought to test a belief for meaning or an argument for validity is an important part of how we will progress in our study.

Defining *reason* also helps us in thinking about the dichotomy between reason and religion that persists in American thought. We will be examining this in more detail as we go, but here, it is important to notice at the start that *reason* and *religion* are often posed as in conflict when *reason* means something other than the laws of thought used formatively and critically. *Reason* can mean thinking confined to the material or physical world, it can mean common sense, or it can mean intuition. In each case, it is set in contrast to *religion*, which usually means either beliefs based on scripture or beliefs about the afterlife.

We will continue to think of reason as the laws of thought and its formative and critical uses while recognizing that it is also used to interpret experience and to construct a worldview. Limiting it to these last two uses is common and will be seen in many of the thinkers we consider. Similarly, we will first be thinking of religion as natural religion or what can be known from general revelation. General revelation is what all persons can know at all times. Scriptures, or special revelation, assume that some things can be known from general revelation. Some of the significant conflicts we will consider in American history involve attempting to give a definition to religion. As *religion* is increasingly defined in a way that includes the religions of the world, as opposed to those that have special revelation, it is understood to involve the use of our basic beliefs to interpret experience. This definition is not in conflict with reason; reason is used to form beliefs and, therefore, reason is fundamental to religion. Religious beliefs can be tested for meaning. Religious beliefs must be tested for meaning because the goal of basic beliefs is to give meaning to experience. One of the first challenges after the American Revolution was about whether special revelation is necessary or if natural religion is sufficient.

We will also notice patterns or repeating dichotomies in American thought. These stretch to early conflicts in New England between the Old Side and New Side in the First Great Awakening. Roughly these involve the conflict between tradition and form on the one hand and personal experience on the other. They continue in a similar pattern as Americans work through the influence of stoic thinking about virtue and epicurean thinking about happiness. And again, these are seen in the Second Great Awakening between the Old School and the New School. They come down to the present as tradition and personal experience continue to be dichotomies: ways of thinking about how to organize individual life, religious life, and political life. They are sometimes expressed as a conflict between common sense and intuition. In each case, reason is used interpretively and constructively but not critically to identify presuppositions behind interpretations and constructions.

THE DECLARATION OF INDEPENDENCE AND THE CONSTITUTION

The Declaration of Independence has been contrasted with the Constitution by some as a Christian or at least Deist document, whereas the Constitution is merely secular. This is because the

Constitution does not contain an explicit reference to God. The Constitution begins with "we the people" as the source of authority without grounding this in the reality of God the Creator. However, others have seen this in reverse and argued that the Declaration is a typical secular Enlightenment document, whereas the Constitution with its checks and balances relies on Christian teachings about the fallen nature of humans and the need for taking this into account when framing a government.

The Declaration of Independence claims that it is self-evident that humans are created. It is that portion of the document that composes the heart of this book. Although it has played many roles in American history, it is the object of study here for three reasons. First, we will consider how it attempts to articulate a foundation for law and society. Second, we will study its specific claims about knowledge, God, and who God is and how these have been challenged and modified from the time of its writing. Third, we will look at the relationship among these truths, law, and authority in the United States. The conclusion from these is that law, even when considered secular, rests on claims about knowledge and about human nature in its relation to what is good and ultimate. Although God is no longer taken to be the metaphysical absolute in the way that the Declaration of Independence views God, there is of necessity another metaphysical absolute put in the place of God. If progress is to be made in overcoming long-standing disputes both in society and about the laws that govern society, then unity must be reached about knowledge, knowing God, and what is good.

Part of what makes the claims of the Declaration of Independence important is that they are said to be knowable by all. Foundational truths about God, humans, and what is good must be knowable if humans are responsible for knowing them and applying them in society and law. Challenges to what can be known are challenges that call into question not only the foundation but also what humans are responsible for knowing and doing. The Declaration of Independence implies that there are some things all humans should know about God and human by stating that these things are self-evident. To fail to know such things is called culpable ignorance.

THE ETHICS OF BELIEF

What ought I believe? This can be answered by thinking about what I should not believe. Some beliefs are false, and I can and should know this. However, it can also be a question about what I ought to know. I cannot be responsible for knowing everything. And some truths cannot be known by all persons or cannot be known without significant study. So this question can also be understood to ask about what are the most basic things that every person ought to know. If it is self-evident that humans are created, then this is something all persons can and should know. Taken from the reverse perspective, if God or the good cannot be known, then humans cannot be held responsible for knowing these things. Therefore, our study about foundational truths for law and society, and indeed for the good life, involves asking what humans can be responsible for knowing.

In my earlier book, *The Ethics of Belief After the Enlightenment*, I proposed the principle of clarity. This states that if something is not clear or not knowable, then humans cannot be held responsible for knowing it. This can be further articulated by the work of Surrendra Gangadean on clarity and basic beliefs. In his book *Philosophical Foundation: A Critical Analysis of Basic Beliefs*, he begins by saying (1) some things are clear; (2) the basic things are clear; and (3) the basic things about God and man and good and evil are clear to reason.[2]

We can understand the truth of each of these by considering their opposite. If nothing is clear, then this includes the claim that nothing is clear. It includes anything I say or think. If the basic things are not clear, then nothing that presupposes the basic things can be clear. And the basic things involve beliefs about what is eternal (God) and what is not (creation, humans), what is good and what is not good. We make distinctions between eternal and noneternal, good and nongood, through the use of reason.

The alternative to affirming that the basic things about God and man and good and evil are clear is nihilism. This is a total nihilism, a denial of all meaning and any distinction, including that of being and nonbeing. This nihilism is both ontologically and existentially impossible. It cannot be the case that there is no distinction between being and nonbeing, nor can one live as if there is no distinction between good and evil (nongood).

Gangadean also gives examples of how presuppositions work and, therefore, how basic beliefs operate in our thinking. Truth presupposes meaning. What is meaningless cannot be true. We interpret our experiences in light of our basic beliefs. Our beliefs about what is finite and temporal presuppose beliefs about what is infinite and eternal. Our beliefs about what is good presuppose our beliefs about human nature.[3] In order to know what is good we must first know human nature (what it is to be a human). This pattern of presuppositions will be present in our study of how American law has made decisions that presuppose beliefs about God, the good, and human nature.

We can see how the Declaration of Independence lays out the basic beliefs that are meant to be known by all and serve as the basis for the new nation. In the famous sentence about what is self-evident, we are given beliefs about God, human nature, and what is good.

There is a sense in which any society or government is grounded on such beliefs whether they are made explicit or not, whether and to what extent they can be articulated or made consistent. What makes the American Revolution stand out is that it made these explicit and that they included the claim that there is God the Creator. The United States and its history can and have been analyzed from many perspectives. But in this one, it is unique. It takes as a starting point a claim that God is knowable and that knowing God is part of knowing what is basic in human society.

The extent to which this foundation of basic beliefs was correctly articulated and understood and the ways in which it has been challenged since that time are the history that we will be considering. In order to do so, we will look at some of the influences on these claims and at some of the notable thinkers after this time that gave formative explanations of God and what is good. I do not claim that this is an exhaustive study of all thinkers that can or should be looked at. And the thinkers I do consider might be important because of their influence, or it might be that their thoughts were the expression of the currents of their day. But I have selected figures that I believe were formative and give us a sense of how belief in God the Creator and how God is known has been challenged and changed.

GOD, KNOWLEDGE, AND THE HUMAN GOOD

The Declaration of Independence stated the foundational beliefs that explained both why the colonies were striking out on their own and what would serve as their unifying principles. These were stated succinctly and needed to be expanded. The Constitution provided the frame of government that would rely on this foundation together with the Bill of Rights that would protect freedom. Jointly, these create a source of unity that would provide the means for keeping together all of the diversity that existed in the early Republic and has increased down to the present. The reality of both unity and diversity raises questions about how to preserve unity while working together within the reality of human differences. Division, which is different from diversity, arises as a critique of the unifying principles that hold a group together. Since the foundational statement in the Declaration of Independence involves claims about God, divisions about the existence and nature of God call into question what unites the system.

In the *Federalist Papers*, Madison argues that separation of church and state and preservation of a union under a constitution involve the use of faction against faction. The Bill of Rights protects against any one faction taking away the liberty of another by becoming a majority. This means that the subject of division between factions cannot be about the necessary foundation for civil government. It must be over secondary issues that do not threaten that Constitution or Bill of Rights. That the factions remain indicates that humans cannot know the actual solution to the division that would bring about unity. This could be either because the subject itself is unknowable or because humans are such that they cannot overcome the divisions even though knowledge is available and possible.

To think about what would count as a basic division and what counts as secondary divisions requires knowing how to relate beliefs to each other as more and less basic. There are basic beliefs in the psychological sense. These are what a given person believes are most important. However, here we are speaking about logically basic beliefs. A basic belief is what is presupposed by other beliefs, and the most basic beliefs are those that are presupposed by all other beliefs in a worldview. They involve the most basic questions that can be asked.

The Declaration of Independence gets to these in making statements about what is real, how we know, and what is of highest value.

Freedom in itself is not the good. Some would say that whatever free persons do is good. However, insofar as a free person has choices, it is possible that the wrong choice can be made. There is a sense in which all humans are free even when they live in a place that does not have political freedom. This is illustrated in the case of Socrates. He serves as the father figure of philosophy. He was free, in the sense that all persons are free, to raise questions about how we know what is good. His inquiry led him into conflict with the rulers of Athens, who charged him with teaching gods other than those the city recognized and of corrupting the youth. In terms of their opposition to him, Socrates was not politically free to pursue his questioning. However, he had a fundamental human freedom to do so and was willing to accept the consequence of capital punishment rather than end his pursuit of wisdom.

Political freedom, and even the freedom that all persons have, is not itself the highest good but is a means to knowing and doing what is good. There is an inherent freedom that all humans possess to pursue what is good. Political freedom allows room to study basic questions but does not guarantee that humans will pursue what is good. From the political perspective, this is the best that can be given. A hierarchical structure or totalitarian regime that requires belief does nothing to advance actual belief or understanding. But the limits of a government that provides freedom become obvious when people do not pursue what is actually good. This indicates that other institutions besides the government must also be operating and healthy in order to teach and encourage pursuit of the good. The government is not total over these other institutions, nor can it define them away. It also indicates that in spite of all institutions, there is the human propensity not to pursue the good, which is itself an indication of the human condition in relation to the good and the need for redemption from the failure to seek, understand, and do what is right.

The question is not whether we are free but what we will do with our freedom. Granting that humans always choose what they perceive to be good, there still remains the problem of knowing if what appears to be good is actually good. Freedom alone cannot tell us this. We might say that only in the context of political freedom can persons come to know the good. However, I believe this confuses inherent freedom with political freedom. Humans in all ages can come to know what is good and are free to question even what a dictatorial government requires them to believe. Political freedom removes some of the obstacles to pursuing the good but does not guarantee that humans will use this political freedom to do so.

As we begin this study, I would like to articulate what I will call the principle of unity. It says:

> **(Principle of Unity) If unity can be achieved about the most basic questions humans can ask, then unity can be achieved on less basic questions that presuppose what is basic.**

The problem both for the American Founders and for us today is in articulating and securing the foundational truths necessary for the unity needed for life together. This unity protects the reality of human diversity but is attacked as divisions arise over what is actually true at the basic level.

This principle relates to the earlier principle of clarity. If nothing is clear, then this includes anything we say or think and is nihilism. The alternative is that some things are clear. It is these things on which we can have unity. They must be the most basic things, because all else presupposes what is most basic. If we cannot have unity on the most basic things, then we cannot have unity on anything that presupposes these; we have no common ground to proceed together.

Something is clear if we can distinguish it from its opposite. We can distinguish God from non-God, human from nonhuman, and the good from what is nongood. There are disagreements about each of these, and we will see in the following study that in each case, there is a denial that there is anything clear, and instead the position of philosophical skepticism is adopted about God and the good. However, if we have the hope of unity, then we must come to know what is clear about God and the good. If something is clear about God and the good, then we can show what is clear. We are responsible to know what is clear and to be able to show what is clear. If we do not know what is clear, then this is a form of culpable ignorance.

THE SELF-EVIDENT AND LAW

In his afterword to the 2012 book *Self-Evident Truths?*, Samuel Moyn asks "What could it mean to hold individual human rights to be 'self-evident' truths, as insurgent Americans famously did in breaking away from the British empire? And why, in the Enlightenment, for the first time, did a group of humans proclaim self-evident human rights as the first premise of their politics, and why is it still that of so many people today?"[4] This quote illustrates a missing piece in research about the Declaration of Independence. In most of the books about the political philosophy of the Declaration of Independence, this is the kind of question that is asked. The question of human rights is the topic of numerous books each year. The idea of rights has greatly expanded since the time of the American Revolution. It is the topic of much international debate, both in theory and in practice.

However, we can question the premise that the Americans began their political quest with a proclamation about human rights. Rather, the actual beginning of this sentence in the Declaration makes a claim about it being self-evident that God created men equal. Within this claim is the idea that some things are self-evident, and the role of God the Creator is one of them. Little or no attention is paid to this portion of the sentence. However, the structure of this central claim in the Declaration follows the formal pattern of relying on an epistemology (some things are self-evident), making a metaphysical claim (God created men equal), and then making its ethical claim that gets all of the attention (there are inalienable human rights).

In the following, we will study the idea of self-evident truths, their origins in Common Sense Philosophy, and their impact on law. We will see how the claims of the Declaration about God and human nature eventually became overlooked or replaced by reliance on intuition and naturalism. This had important consequences for law in the United States. Not only that, this study will show that the multiplication of new religious movements in the nineteenth and twentieth centuries increasingly required that claims about self-evident truths concerning God be ignored from a political and legal perspective. Increasing divisions about these foundational beliefs undermined the ability to have unity at the basic level.

The current approach is to overlook these differences about belief in God and how God is known and instead focus on human rights. I will argue that this approach will not and cannot work, and that instead we must bring into relief the different foundations for these systems of law. Even when God and how God is known are not explicitly made a part of law, there are implicit assumptions about these matters. This is true even when the assumption is that there is no God or that God is not active in human affairs or that if there is a God, there is no knowledge of God, only opinion.

Finally, we will consider contemporary applications of law, the "hot-button" decisions that continue to divide our country. My argument will be that the Declaration of Independence asserted that some things about God and human nature are self-evident and that if this claim is taken seriously, it will go a long way to resolving disputes that continue to divide. In either case, decisions about these kinds of cases make assumptions about God and the knowledge of God.

THE DECLARATION AND FOUNDATION

"Basic human rights lie right at the centre of our core values in Western society today."[5] This quote summarizes how the Declaration of Independence is studied. Indeed, in contrast to the Declaration of Independence, the U.N.'s Declaration of Universal Human Rights overlooks any mention of God and simply starts with assertions about rights. The Declaration of Independence stands out as unique not only because of its significant impact in world history but because of how it begins. In our current study, we will fill this gap and provide much-needed research on what can arguably be said to be the most important claims in the Declaration of Independence.

The Declaration of Independence has been studied from almost every perspective imaginable. So, too, have the lives and political philosophies of the principle contributors to that document. The present study will contribute to this by looking at the Declaration as a creed that sets forth the basic beliefs of the nation and studying how these were understood and challenged in the time since the Revolution.

Although the Declaration of Independence is held in high esteem, it makes a startling claim that few today would actually accept. This is that some things are self-evident, and among these are that humans are created. From the claim that this Creator endows humans with rights, we can infer that this is a personal creator along the lines of theism or deism. And yet, if God exists, is it self-evident that God exists? In the following, I will explore this question and its importance for both religion and law in the United States.

Although events were already set in motion for a revolution by the time the Declaration of Independence was written, it states the founding ideas that serve to explain the origin of the new country. It is written to the world to explain why the colonists decided on independence. In order to justify their decision, it gives principles that it takes to be basic and universal. These are its claims about what is self-evident, about God and human nature, and about human rights and the pursuit of what is good.

RELIGIOUS FREEDOM

The American Revolution and the Declaration of Independence occur in the middle of a longer account about religion and freedom:

> The American revolution of religion actually began forty years before the Declaration of Independence during the Great Awakening, evangelical revivalists defied civil and ecclesiastical authority to preach the message of the New Birth without regard to existing institutions and laws. They ignored parish boundaries, preaching wherever people gathered. They allowed lay exhorters to preach, bypassing church boards that licensed ministers. And they continued to dispatch unlicensed itinerants on preaching tours after legislatures passed regulations to curb such activity. Empowered by their New Birth experiences, many laypersons rejected the authority of pastors they deemed to be "unconverted," removed themselves from established congregations, and formed their own Separate churches ... Whether Churchmen or Dissenters, all Patriots united in resisting British attempts to curb their religious freedom.[6]

The idea of religious freedom is at the heart of the original colonies. Even Jamestown, which is usually thought to be merely a profit-seeking venture, was part of the larger conflict between Protestant England and Catholic Spain and France. By the time of the Revolution, the Congregationalists and Anglicans had been joined by Dissenters. The founders were concerned to avoid the religious strife and wars that had ravaged Europe. One of the ways that they sought to do this was to give religious freedom rather than requiring subscription to a state religion.

> With Jefferson and Madison leading the legislative fight, most historians have credited them with winning the battle for religious freedom. However, they themselves recognized that their success would have been impossible without the thousands of Dissenters who over the previous forty years had poured into the state, many of them emigrating from Pennsylvania. Jefferson noted that by 1776 a majority of Virginians were Dissenters.[7]

The problem for organizing a republic was the need for a virtuous citizenry. However, if there were competing beliefs about what is good, then there would be endless divisions. The imposition of order from the top down had not avoided war or given unity. People were willing to violate the law to keep their conscience and beliefs about what is good. The solution decided upon by the Founders was to use this propensity for divisions to secure a kind of peace.

> The delegates knew that social concord in a republic depended on a virtuous citizenry, but the question was how to ensure public virtue. The Puritan Fathers had believed that God through divine Election produced men who could be trusted with the franchise and office holding. Leaders of the Great Awakening had agreed, emphasizing the necessity of a spiritual conversion to transform willful, selfish people into obedient servants of God and man. Though many delegates expressed their belief that religious instruction promotes morality and thus good citizenship, few had faith that religion alone would produce virtuous citizens ... In the end, the delegates agreed with Madison that men and women could not be relied upon to act always as virtuous citizens. But they could be relied upon to act out of self-interest, and the great diversity

> of competing interests presented a fair prospect of preventing any one interest from oppressing the others.[8]

Protestantism had in its history the affirmation of the freedom of conscience. However, as divisions grew among the Protestants, the hope for unity in the church was lost. Without that unity, it was not obvious how there could be unity in the state. Rather than work for this unity first, the Founders encouraged the idea of competition between groups within the context of the state.

> With almost unanimous consent, the Founders agreed, going beyond the planters' notion of religious liberty: the "Protestant sense of liberation from the shackles of Rome (or in the case of an independent America, Canterbury)." Rather, they embraced the "liberal idea of free competition among a variety of sects ... qualified by concern lest liberty degenerate into license."[9]

This promised stability in the midst of differences about what is good.

> The centrifugal force of myriad sectarian interests, it was feared, would render futile any attempt at defining a common faith. The Founders were more optimistic, believing that a free, competitive religious market would both ensure religious vitality and prevent religious wars. In other words, they believed that religious liberty, not religious regulation, was the more effective bond in a pluralistic society.[10]

This approach still requires a framework in which liberty will operate. The concern that liberty not degenerate into license assumes that there is some check to that process. The Declaration of Independence provides the outlines of such a framework by giving the basics that will serve as common ground in the operation of the government and unity in society.

COMMON GROUND

Common ground is what is taken for granted as the background for getting along and continuing life together. What is common ground is the same for all persons. It is universal, and it is knowable. There is a responsibility to know what is common ground, and ignorance of this is no excuse. It is culpable ignorance.

The Declaration of Independence gives what it takes to be common ground in each of the areas of epistemology, metaphysics, and ethics. It makes the assertion that we can know because it affirms what is self-evident. The failure to know what is self-evident is inexcusable. However, misidentifying what is self-evident will result in a failure to have common ground built on a lasting foundation. We will see the common ground stated in the Declaration of Independence challenged in the centuries following its writing. These challenges call into question whether God can be known and in what sense it can be said there is a creator at all.

The idea that we can begin with what is self-evident and knowable is in contrast to skepticism and fideism. Skepticism says that we cannot know. It says that there are only competing opinions and that all opinions are equal. Fideism agrees that we cannot know but says that we must believe something. Fideism can come in varying degrees, from the bald affirmation of blindly believing to accepting a belief that seems more plausible than its competitors while not yet counting as knowledge.

In contrast to skepticism and fideism, the Declaration of Independence affirms that there are foundational truths and that they can be known. The history of the United States is one of testing and challenging the foundation in the Declaration of Independence and revealing its shortcomings. These challenges begin with a rejection of the idea that anything is self-evident and then continue to the idea of God the Creator.

At the time of its writing, atheism was rare. Deism, belief in God the creator but not ruler, was becoming popular in some circles. Yet even among Theists who believed that God is both the creator and the ruler, there were divisions about the nature of God. These divisions included disagreements about what it meant for God to be sovereign, about God's plan of salvation and how redemption is applied and accomplished, and about how God acts to bring about the triumph of good over evil. These are traceable to disagreements about how to know God, about what is the highest good, and about the role of natural evil in history.

Given these disagreements about the nature of God, we can anticipate that the use of the term "creator" in the Declaration is ambiguous. Minimally, it refers to God the creator and to nature's God, so as to distinguish it from atheism, from dualism (God organizes but does not create), and from pantheism (the belief that all is God and, therefore, there is no creation and no creator). Beyond this, it seems to offer only a vague idea of God that is agreeable to either deism or theism and that does not address the various divisions among theists mentioned earlier.

It could be thought that more precision is not necessary for this kind of document. It is sufficient to relate God to man and human rights without giving more information. To understand why this is not the case, we need to think about the relationship between God, the good, and law. Ultimately, the Declaration is arguing that the actions of the colonists are "legal" or "just" in relation to a natural law that governs all nations and people. Obviously their actions are "illegal" from the perspective of English law. Therefore, the Declaration appeals to a higher law, a law that is the standard of judgment above any national law. It references this in the phrase "the Laws of Nature and Nature's God."

Metaphysics is the study of what is real. Not all descriptions of reality support the idea of a natural moral law. For instance, if pantheism is the true account of reality and all is God (all is one), then good and evil are both part of God. In the attempt to separate church and state, there has been a continued attempt to keep the state out of the arena of personal beliefs about what is real. However, the state itself assumes some things about reality and about what it is to have a good society. It makes assumptions about human nature and how humans resolve disputes. In this way, metaphysics is inseparable from law and the state.

Why not consider the assertion that some things are self-evident and that among these are the existence of a Creator, a kind of rhetorical flourish? For practical purposes, this seems to be how it has been read. The great weight of emphasis has been on the ideas of equality and human rights. However, the idea that the claim is a mere rhetorical addition to the rest of the document, which is to be taken at its word, sets a strange juxtaposition between this sentence and the arguments advanced in the body of the work. Those arguments take the ideas of self-evidence, human nature, equality, and rights as supporting premises in their argument.

There is also the relationship among claims about human rights, human nature, and the origin of human nature. In philosophy, these are called the areas of ethics, metaphysics, and epistemology. The claim that there are human rights is a claim about ethics, about how humans ought to live. As such, it presupposes what it is to be a human and what is good for a human. A significant part of understanding what it is to be a human is understanding the origin of human nature. Competing theories of origins give competing views of what it is to be a human. Therefore, the assertion that humans are created, and created equal, is a bold claim about the origin of humanity. The reality of human nature and the Creator are part of the study of metaphysics.

Presupposed in these claims about ethics and metaphysics is epistemology. This is the study of knowledge. How do we know about human nature and God? The Declaration of Independence takes the position that some things are self-evident. We will look at this idea in more detail. At this point, we can see that this famous sentence follows the pattern of giving an epistemology that supports a metaphysics, which in turn supports an ethical theory. To study this presuppositionally, we must begin with the first step in that chain and ask what it means for something to be self-evident.

SELF-EVIDENT AND SELF-ATTESTING

In order to set the context for thinking about what is self-evident, we have taken time to consider reason and the relationships between beliefs. We can wonder what the intended meaning of the term "self-evident" was. Was it intended to mean that these are beliefs the authors and signatories took to be obvious? Because the Declaration is a document written to the world, giving arguments to justify the actions of the colonists, any reading that says this is just a statement about what the authors believed must be incorrect. It is part of an argument intended for the world to read.

Perhaps we could read "self-evident" to mean common sense or common consent. These beliefs are things that the authors and signers believed everyone agreed on or are at least things that everyone in the colonies agreed on. Although it might be true that they were commonly held beliefs, since they are used to justify the actions of the colonists to the world, they must be more than that. The Declaration is stating that what the colonists are doing is reasonable because it follows from premises that are also reasonable. The premises must be more than what the colonists hold or else their argument becomes self-centered: what we are doing is reasonable because we think it is reasonable. Instead, these claims are premises that are meant to be agreed upon by everyone.

Therefore, "self-evident" seems to mean something that everyone will take to be self-evident. This requires an examination of what it means for something to be self-evident. This is perhaps the most difficult part of the sentence. The authors and signers of the Declaration of Independence were not ignorant of the fact that some people did not believe in a creator. Nor were they ignorant of the many theistic proofs of God's existence that had been given by philosophers over the centuries. To claim both that there is a creator and that this is self-evident requires work to understand.

For an idea or belief to be self-evident means that once the concepts are grasped, the truth of the belief is understood. The best examples of what is self-evident are the laws of thought. These are identity, excluded middle, and noncontradiction. The law of identity says: *a* is *a*. The law of excluded middle says: either *a* or *non-a*. The law of noncontradiction says: not both *a* and *non-a*. These three are all interconnected and are restatements of the act of grasping the concept *a*. Once we understand that whatever something is, that's what it is, we also understand that it isn't what it isn't. Simply understanding the concepts involved is enough to understand the truth of these claims.

Some might want to distinguish between what is self-evident and what is self-attesting. What is self-evident could refer to what appears to be true to a given person. In this sense, people can disagree about what is self-evident. By way of contrast, something is self-attesting when it proves itself. Something is self-attesting when it establishes the basis for thought itself; therefore, it cannot be questioned because it makes questioning possible. We have seen and will continue to study how reason as the laws of thought is self-attesting. However, what the Declaration of Independence claims to be self-evident is not self-attesting. Because of this, it left the door open for significant divisions about what it claimed to be foundational.

This is in contrast to claiming that the senses give us what is self-evident. Our senses are immediate in that they give us information such as sight, sound, or feeling directly and not by inference. However, this information must be interpreted, and, once we do that, we are entering into an area that is not self-evident but can be debated. Do the senses give us information of a material world that exists outside of all minds? Or do the senses give us information about ideas that exist either in our mind or in God's mind? These are two different interpretations of the information from our senses that have been debated in the history of philosophy. So we can distinguish between what is immediate but in need of interpretation and what is self-evident.

What is self-evident is also in contrast to what is sometimes called intuition. "Intuition" is a broadly used term and could mean whatever is given immediately. In this way, it could apply to the senses. But it is also used in a narrower sense to refer to the relationship between signs and reality. Someone might say he/she "felt" as if something bad were going to happen. This sign, a feeling, is thought to have some relationship to reality. However, there is not always a relationship between such a sign and reality. Nor is this relationship self-evident.

What is self-evident can also be in contrast to what is taken to be common sense. Common sense takes the condition of the perceiver for granted as if it were absolute. It assumes that appearance is reality without questioning how the perceiver understands appearance. However, what is common sense to one person or one group is not always common sense to another person or another group. As such, this is not the same as what is self-evident. Whatever is actually self-evident is self-evident for everyone who understands the concepts involved.

Hopefully this allows us to isolate what is actually self-evident and avoid ambiguously relating it to the senses, intuition, or common sense. Having done this, we can ask if it really is self-evident that all men are created equal. Or if it is self-evident that there is a creator in the first place. In doing this, we see how the Declaration relies on the relationship between human nature and human origins. This cannot merely be a claim that humans are equal because not all accounts of human origins support the claim that humans are equal. The idea here is that humans are equal as creatures made in the image of God.

That there is God the Creator is not self-evident in the way that the laws of thought are self-evident. It is in making this assertion that the Declaration of Independence opens itself up to criticism and reinterpretation. A critic can say that it is not self-evident that God exists and from there object to the beliefs that are supported by God the Creator, such as equality and human rights. A reinterpretation can be given that understands the idea of God in a different sense than is meant by theism. We will see both of these occur as U.S. history unfolds.

METHODOLOGY

In the following study, there will be a historical as well as a philosophical methodology. The historical approach will be a consideration of challenges that have been raised to the idea of God and how God is known. These challenges elicit responses that in turn bring about further challenges. Tracing this process will take us from the writing of the Declaration of Independence to the present day. It will explain how we have arrived at our current understanding of what is self-evident and what created human nature.

The philosophical methodology will be to critically examine these challenges and their responses [for meaning]. A challenge presses believers to examine their assumptions for meaning. When assumptions are exposed as meaningless, a response will be made to try and retain meaning. We will trace how people seek to obtain meaning and preserve the meaning of their beliefs in the face of challenges. As the meaninglessness of beliefs is exposed, people will change their beliefs about what is good for other goods that they believe will bring satisfaction. In the case of believers, this is often the idea of heaven, where happiness is attained in the afterlife. In the case of atheists, this is often the idea of maximizing pleasure in this life.

The combination of this historical and philosophical approach will allow us to critically analyze where we are today in our thinking about God and the knowledge of God. Has a new insight about the creator of human nature been discovered? Or has something else been put in the place of what is self-evident? Or, instead, have beliefs about these matters been set aside in the hopes of pleasure either in this life or in heaven? The challenge to basic beliefs about what is self-evident, what is real, and what is the highest good requires greater consistency in these areas if the good is to be realized in the lives of individuals and society.

PHILOSOPHY AND BASIC BELIEFS TODAY

Today it is taken for granted that there are not many truths that are self-evident and that those that are do not give us much information. We can consider Alvin Plantinga, who is perhaps the most famous Christian philosopher of the last few decades. He says, "the central truths of Christianity are not self-evident, nor, so far as anyone can see, are they such that they can be deduced from what is self-evident."[11]

He critiques what many have come to call the Enlightenment view of knowledge. This view says that we must begin with what is self-evident or incorrigible (what we cannot help believing) or evident to the senses. He says: "Evidentialism is the view that belief in God is rationally justifiable or acceptable only if there is *good evidence* for it, where good evidence would be arguments from other propositions one knows. If it is accepted apart from such evidence or arguments, then it is at best intellectually third-rate: irrational, or unreasonable, or contrary to one's intellectual obligations."[12] And: "Let's say, a bit vaguely, that according to classical foundationalists, a proposition is properly basic, for a person S, if and only if it is self-evident for S, or incorrigible for S, or evident to the senses for S."[13]

The argument that he and others use to reject what they call evidentialism is that we cannot get much information by starting with these standards. Also, if we require an argument to support our beliefs, then we will require an argument to support that argument, and so on. We cannot simply rely on reason, because we will need to give support for reason.

> Even if we could give an argument to show that a given source of belief was, in fact, reliable, in making that argument we would be obliged to rely on *other* sources of beliefs. In particular, we would

> have to rely on reason; but clearly we can't establish that reason is reliable without relying on reason itself; so beliefs that are produced by reason are uncredentialed.[14]

If we take this approach, we end up with some arguments in favor of belief in God and other arguments against belief in God:

> Considering the *arguments* for and against the existence of God. On the pro side, there were the traditional theistic proofs, the cosmological, teleological, and ontological arguments, to follow Kant's classification. On the con side, there was, first of all, the problem of evil (construed as the claim that the existence of evil is logically inconsistent with the existence of a wholly good, all-powerful, and all-knowing God). Then there were also some rather opaque claims to the effect that the progress of modern science, or the attitudes necessary to its proper pursuits, or perhaps something similar lurking in the nearby bushes, or maybe something else that had been learned by 'man come of age'–the idea was that something in this general neighborhood also offers evidence against the existence of God. And it was also clearly assumed that belief in God was rational and proper only if on balance the evidence, so construed, favored it.[15]

However, the Enlightenment view says that we should not believe anything for which we do not have good reasons. This is our rational duty.

> And his [Locke's] answer, as we have seen, is that a rational creature in our circumstances ought to govern his opinions by reason – that is, proportion his belief to what is certain for him. But how are we to understand the "may" and "ought" and "should" that Locke employs in stating his project? ... his words have a *deontological* ring; they are redolent of duty, obligation, permission, being within your rights and the rest of the deontological stable.[16]

Another philosopher who also argues for an externalist approach is Michael Bergmann. An externalist approach is one that considers knowledge claims from the third-person perspective rather than the first-person, or internalist, perspective. In such an account the issue is whether a person is warranted to hold beliefs from their senses, whether these are senses of the external world or internal experiences like religious experiences. In this way, it is an empiricist account of knowledge. It assumes that knowledge is from experience and then seeks to respond to skeptical challenges to empiricism. The standard skeptical challenges are that perhaps we are being fooled or tricked by an evil demon or mad scientist about what we are experiencing.

Like Plantinga, Bergmann offers a theory of warrant to explain when a person has knowledge from experience. The person need not be aware or able to prove that they have knowledge. Thus the title of his book *Justification without Awareness*. Instead, a description of the conditions of knowledge is given and holds whether the person knows it or not. This is a kind of sociological description of knowledge rather than the traditional question of epistemology, "how do I know?"

Just as Plantinga raised problems with the standards of the Enlightenment for knowledge, so, too, Bergmann raises challenges for the standard of what he calls strong awareness. He says,

> The claim to be defended here is that a strong awareness requirement on justification gives rise to vicious regress problems leading to radical skepticism. Strong awareness, you will recall, is awareness that involves conceiving of the justification-contributor that is the object of awareness as being in some way relevant to the truth or justification of the relevant belief."[17]

He notes two kinds of regress. One is that the requirement that a person believe that they have justification requires a further belief about that belief stretching to infinity. The other is that the justification of each belief requires an ever-increasing complexity that is implausible.[18]

Bergmann gives a definition of objectivity: the fittingness of doxastic response B to evidence E is objective fittingness (in the sense that fittingness from the subject's perspective isn't sufficient for it).[19] He relies on Thomas Reid to consider the difference between learned and unlearned doxastic responses to sensations. Could the information we now receive from texture or smell have instead given us some other information? The examples considered by Bergmann and Reid are very specifically empirical examples of ordinary objects. As such, it is not clear that they help us in our question about whether it is self-evident that God the creator exists.

Plantinga said that it is not. Instead, he relies on an account of religious experience that uses an externalist account of warrant.

However, his account includes the idea of a design plan aimed at truth, which seems to import the idea of God. This becomes circular as it stands: we are warranted to believe in God because God designed us that way. However, it could be modified as a way of arguing that knowledge is not possible apart from such a design plan (knowledge requires the existence of God). This is no longer an externalist account of knowledge but is an internalist argument about how we can know that God exists. Indeed, externalism is supported and defended by internalist arguments about how we can know externalist accounts are true. As such, internalist answers to the problem "how do I know?" are unavoidable.

Bergmann relies on Reid to say that it is a first principle that our faculties are reliable.[20]

> Just as we have non-inferential knowledge about our immediate physical environment by means of sense perception and about our past by means of memory and about our own minds by means of introspection, so also we have a faculty by means of which we have non-inferential knowledge of first principles. Reid thinks of first principles as self-evident truths. He thinks some are contingent and some are necessary. The one mentioned above (concerning the reliability of our natural faculties) is contingent. And the faculty by which we know these first principles (whether necessary or contingent) he calls "common sense."[21]

Bergmann clarifies Reid's term "common sense." He says,

> His intention is to include only propositions that almost everyone believes (and knows) non-inferentially – things that are immediately accepted by sane persons once considered and understood. That 2+2=4, that modus ponens is a valid form of inference, that the thoughts of which I am conscious are my thoughts, that I have some degree of control over my actions – these are examples of what Reid considers the dictates of common sense. The first two are examples of necessary truths known by common sense; the latter two are contingent truths.[22]

How do we know the deliverances of common sense? Reid articulates what he calls the emotion of ridicule. "On the basis of this experience, we do two things: we dismiss as absurd the contrary of the first principle and we believe the first principle itself. Thus, non-inferential common sense beliefs, like non-inferential perceptual beliefs, are based on experiential evidence."[23] Bergmann believes this account is more realistic than accounts that require an argument to support believing our senses or noninferential judgments.

Bergmann says that "a person's beliefs are justified if and only if they satisfy the proper function and no-defeater conditions."[24] Bergmann considers whether his account can be used by a fanatic to justify any ridiculous religious belief. However, he does not consider the many beliefs of the world's religions that one should not call fanatical. Under the conditions described, people can and have arrived at nontheistic positions, and religions have been believed that span millennia and influence billions of people. These kinds of beliefs can appeal to these same standards and cannot be dismissed as fanatical. Still considering the fanatic, he says, "What it does mean is that we must give up on the false hope that playing by the rules of proper philosophical exchange will enable us to resolve all serious disagreements about matters such as fanatical religious views."[25] But what about nonfanatical views of the world's religions? We will consider many competing views of "God" in the next chapters that can all appeal to these same standards.

CONCLUSION

Considering Plantinga and Bergmann has helped us see where epistemology is today. Plantinga and Bergmann treat belief in God as a matter of experience and warrant concerning our beliefs about experience. They both rely on accounts derived from Thomas Reid and Scottish Common Sense philosophy. This was the philosophy that influenced the Founders and the Declaration of Independence. So it remains for us to see if it is self-evident that God the Creator exists. There are many nontheistic worldviews that reject belief in God but are not the kind of fanatics that Bergmann addresses. Perhaps these can maintain that their nontheistic first principle is self-evident and God the Creator is not.

We are led to Thomas Reid and his ideas of first principles and what is self-evident. Can the Declaration of Independence's claims about what is self-evident be held as such, or must they be abandoned as incorrect? It seems to be the consensus among atheists and Christian philosophers that it is not self-evident that God the Creator exists. Indeed, it seems to be agreed that belief in God does not require arguments and that there are not conclusive arguments. Instead, theists have sought a different standard for support of belief in God. If this is where we are today, how did we get here from the claim that it is self-evident that humans are created equal? This is what we will explore in the following chapters.

1 THOMAS JEFFERSON AND THOMAS PAINE

What does it mean to have religious freedom? How does freedom of conscience relate to toleration? In this chapter we consider these questions by studying what it means to know God. Both Thomas Jefferson and Thomas Paine affirmed that there is a God but rejected the idea that God has given special revelation. This claim by these two thinkers makes religious beliefs grounded in special revelation merely personal opinions at best. How will this influence religious freedom?

Michael McConnell is currently a law professor at Stanford Law School. He has also served as a circuit judge on the U.S. Court of Appeals for the Tenth Circuit. He is a leading authority on the freedom of religion. In summarizing the Supreme Court's approach to religious freedom in the mid-twentieth century, he notes:

> When the Supreme Court began to decide cases in the 1940s involving claims about an establishment of religion, the justices did not make a serious attempt to canvass the legal history of establishment ... The justices focused instead on one event in one state – the rejection of Patrick Henry's Assessment Bill in Virginia in 1785 and the adoption of Thomas Jefferson's alternative Bill for the Establishment of Religious Freedom – on the assumption that "the provisions of the First Amendment ... had the same objective and were intended to provide the same protection against governmental intrusion on religious liberty as the Virginia statute."[1]

In contrast to this limited approach to religious freedom and the establishment clause, he identifies ways that understanding of the establishment clause has changed as it moved from a narrow to a more inclusive interpretation:

> An establishment of religion is the promotion and inculcation of a common set of beliefs through governmental authority. An establishment may be narrow (focused on a particular set of beliefs) or broad (encompassing a certain range of opinion), it may be more or less coercive, and it may be tolerant or intolerant of other views. During the period between initial settlement and ultimate disestablishment, American religious establishments moved from being narrow, coercive, and intolerant to being broad, relatively noncoercive, and tolerant. Although the laws constituting the establishment were ad hoc and unsystematic, they can be summarized in six categories: (1) control over doctrine, governance, and personnel of the church; (2) compulsory church attendance; (3) financial support; (4) prohibitions on worship in dissenting churches; (5) use of church institutions for public functions; and (6) restriction of political participation to members of the established church.[2]

We will see each of these categories in cases we consider. As courts began to hear cases involving religious belief, the separation of church and state was put to the test. Some of these cases involved property or corporate organizations, and as such, the state did have some interest in how the decisions were made. Others involved religious beliefs and practices. In these cases, the state was on less sure ground in making decisions. Some principles began to be articulated in the late twentieth century due to cases such as *Wisconsin v. Yoder* (1972). One of these was whether the religious belief in question was central to the actual religion. This test only lasted a few decades before it was struck down because it put the court in a place to decide the role of beliefs for a religion. In its place, emphasis was placed on the role of the believer to determine the significance of a religious belief or practice. Another change was from the idea of religious toleration to the free exercise of religion.

When the focus was on toleration, the government had a role in determining which religious beliefs or practices to tolerate. An emphasis on free exercise put the importance back on the believers and out of the state's jurisdiction.[3] Here we are going to look back at specific cases as they relate to the subject of each chapter and help highlight how ideas about what is self-evident, the nature of God, and how God is known affected the cases. These cases might simply be thought of in terms of the progressive limitation of the state in matters of religious belief. That is a part of the story. However, since it also involves the idea of the secular, the idea of what is common to all and necessary for life together, which is under the authority of the state, defining "religious" and "secular" becomes of vital importance. In giving such a definition, there is of necessity much being said about God and the knowledge of God.

In 1772, Massachusetts published an antiblasphemy law that was enforced for the next fifty years. This had a Trinitarian basis in that blasphemy against God, Christ, or the Holy Spirit was covered as a violation of the law. A similar law in Virginia, enacted in 1792, resulted in the case *The People Against Ruggles*. The defense in this case maintained that such laws in England are due to the established Church of England and its role in the common law of that state. However, in the United States, there is no established church, and, therefore, blasphemy is not an offense to the common law. The defendant should be free to express his religious opinions. "*Judaism* and *Mahometanism* may be preached here without any legal animadversion. For aught that appears, the prisoner may have been a *Jew*, a *Mahometan*, or a *Socianian*; and if so, he had a right by the constitution to declare his opinions."[4]

The opinion of the court disagreed. Rather than taking this as a case of expressing religious opinions, the offense was one of speaking wickedly, maliciously, and blasphemously in the presence of good and Christian people.[5] The particular phrase was a slur against the birth of Jesus Christ and against the morality of his mother. "The language was blasphemous not only in a popular, but in a legal sense; for blasphemy, according to the most precise definitions, consists in maliciously reviling God, or religion, and this was reviling Christianity through its author."[6] The court maintained that such words were an offense at common law. Citing a previous case (*Rex v. Woolston*), "the court said they would not suffer it to be debated whether defaming Christianity in general was not an offense at common law, for that whatever strikes at the root of Christianity, tends manifestly to the dissolution of civil government. But the court was careful to say, that they did not intend to include disputes between learned men upon particular controverted points."[7] Contemptuous and profane attacks on God, Christ, or the Holy Spirit tend to corrupt the morals of the people and destroy good order.[8] As such, the court claimed that they are not dependent on an established religion but are the basis for civil order, and as such, the state has an essential interest in protecting civil society.

The court maintained: "We stand equally in need, now as formerly, of all that moral discipline, and of those principles of virtue, which help to bind society together ... Nothing could be more offensive to the virtuous part of the community, or more injurious to the tender morals of the young, than to declare such profanity lawful. It would go to confound all distinction between things sacred and profane."[9] The court noted the common law practice of laying a hand on the Bible when taking an oath. "Surely, then, we are bound to conclude, that wicked and malicious words, writings and actions which go to vilify those gospels, continue, as at common law, to be an offence against the public peace and safety."[10]

Another Massachusetts law, from 1782, affirmed the role of the Lord's Day and church attendance for the welfare of the community. The purpose of the Lord's Day was "affording necessary seasons for relaxation from labour and the cares of business; for moral reflections and conversation on the duties of life, and the frequent errors of human conduct; for publick and private worship of the Maker, Governour and Judge of the world, and for those acts of charity which support and adorn a Christian society."[11] Included in the duties of the Lord's Day was the attendance of public worship. A person who is physically able but does not attend public worship for an entire month would be fined. The law does not specify which church must be attended, only that the Lord's Day and church attendance are an important part of the welfare of society.

It is worth noting that the Massachusetts law, when challenged in 1838, was upheld by Unitarians.[12] Therefore, these ideas of blasphemy cannot be reduced to a Trinitarian impulse or favor. Instead, there was the recognition that civil government rested on virtue and that virtue was connected to religion, which included belief in God and the Bible. This was not simply the question of whether there could be a moral atheist. Rather, it was whether there could be an atheist who is able to be moral in a way that is consistent with atheism rather than using a borrowed morality from theism.

TOLERANCE AND FREEDOM

In making this case, the courts were working to include the need for toleration among beliefs while also affirming that some beliefs and practices are necessary for the health of a secular civil society. At this point, there was not thought to be a division or conflict between the idea of religion and the secular. These were two different but supporting spheres of life. These laws were not seen as establishing a religion in the way that the Church of England is the established religion of England. However, it was affirmed that there is a relationship between religion and virtue and between virtue and civil society. As challenges were mounted against this connection, these laws were increasingly challenged. In the following, we will look at how this theory of religion and the secular was understood.

There was not common agreement at the time of the writing of the Declaration of Independence that natural theology had any role to play in knowing God. It appeared to some that appeals to natural theology were introducing non-Christian elements into the Christian message from philosophy and pagan thinkers. And it is true that the Founders were influenced by Roman philosophers like Cicero. This approach is consistent with McConnell's analysis. He says:

> Even in the founding era, however, a principled liberal opposition to establishment was taking shape, mostly among dissident religious groups such as the Baptists and other heirs to the Great Awakening. Their argument against establishment of religion had a decidedly religious cast. It was a usurpation of spiritual authority for political bodies to purport to interpret the Scripture; conviction and conversion were the work of the Holy Spirit, not the legislature.[13]

In other words, the concern was from the religious or theological side and involved a concern about how people change their beliefs and values. From this perspective, the role of the state in that process is minimal at best. McConnell concludes that "It is a mistake, therefore, to view the establishment of religion through the lens of modern preoccupations about whether political society is too infused with religiosity. Establishment was not really about religion; it was about government control over the formation of public opinion."[14]

Instead, the theological and political reasons for disestablishment were grounded in utilitarian concerns about how to promote a moral citizenry. He observes,

> The political rationale treated religion as a means for promoting the civic purposes of the state. It rested on the social utility rather than the truth of religion ... Truth and social utility may, but need not, coincide... The theological rationale can be seen in the earliest colonial charters. There is good reason to suspect, however, that in most places and at most times, the political rationale was generally more influential, at least to those in command of the government. Religion is a key determinant of the values and virtues of a people, and the ability to shape values and virtues is useful to anyone who wishes to rule.[15]

In addition to this, some of the divisions and sects that had appeared, such as the Unitarians, spoke highly about their use of reason and its role in their conclusions. The consequence was confusion about the exact role of natural theology and its scope in the Christian life. The Founders relied on values of the Enlightenment to support their beliefs about God and law. However, not everyone at the time held these values. Some viewed it as a departure from the role of special revelation in the life of society. It was seen as a kind of deism, either explicitly or by implication, because of the role it gave to natural theology. Let us consider some of these objections.

NATURAL RELIGION

The English dissenter Abraham Taylor gave voice to some of these concerns. He saw the emphasis on natural religion as a departure from the doctrines of the Reformation.

> It must be observed, that at the same time that natural religion was talk'd of, to the neglect of the doctrines of revelation, a deluge of Atheism, irreligion and immorality flow'd in upon those of

> the national establishment; and whether since we of the separation have heard so much noise about it, there has not been a declension as to justice and common honesty, a contempt of the Sabbath, and a neglect of public worship, is what every one is able to judge of, who has look'd a little into the world.[16]

So what exactly is *reason* and what is its role in knowing God, the good, and formulating law? Abraham Taylor says:

> No one will be so silly as to say, that reason, in the abstract idea of it, is insufficient and imperfect, for nothing is to be regarded which is contrary to reason. The question is not then, whether reason abstractly consider'd is imperfect, for that would be questioning whether truth is truth, or whether right reason is right reason; which would be only trifling, and sending words to no purpose. True reason is right, and what is right, cannot, as such, be said to be imperfect ... the question really is, whether reason, as it is now in men, whether the light of nature, as it is in men in their present state, which none can venture to say, in fact, is not a state of degeneracy, is a sufficient rule to inform men what they ought to believe and receive, to shew them how they may find out what is true and right, and to direct them in the more private walks of life, as well as when they may have the advantage of seeing the example of others; it is, whether natural religion, of itself, discovers all that a man is to believe concerning God, all the methods necessary for him to take, in order to be reconciled to him, and regain his favour, and all that is required of man in his private, relative, and social character.[17]

This was and is a common view among Christians: that reason is now fallen, cannot be trusted, and, therefore, we need the Bible. This position denies that we can know what is good and moral apart from special revelation. The idea of a natural moral law based on human nature and directed at the good is thought to somehow take away humanity's responsibility to God and make them only responsible to themselves and their own happiness:

> We are told, that the distinction of right and wrong, virtue and vice, is entirely independent of the will of God, and that it arises from the nature of things, by which senseless jargon may be meant fate, chance, the animating soul of the world, without an idea annex'd to it. It is pretended, that men are not made by God for himself and that he has no motive, on his own account, to give them laws, or

> to punish the breach of them, and that consequently they are not accountable to him, but that such fully answer the end of their creation, as contribute all they can to their own and other's happiness. This is to suppose, that God has power to create rational creatures, and it is a favour that this is allow'd, but that he has no authority to prescribe them laws, seeing the rules of justice rise from the nature of things, and he is confined to act by them, as much as those he has created; that he has no justice to glorify when he is provoked, but is obliged to be kind to all his creatures, whether they obey him, or revel against him; in short, that he is an indolent being, such as was the god of the Epicureans; that man is independent of him who created him, and preserves him, and that he is to be his own judge, whether he answers the end of his creation, by promoting his own happiness, and that of others. Thus the irrational stuff, which was hiss'd off the stage, with just contempt, when it was introduced by Epicurus, is afresh brought on, to shew the sufficiency of human reason, in our enlighten'd age of search and enquiry.[18]

Abraham Taylor sees a decline in religious orthodoxy and traces this to the influence of Deists (who appeal to reason) and those Christian ministers who claim to hold to the scriptures but gave the Deists ample ammunition. He names specific Protestant doctrines, important parts of Protestant Reformation, that are no longer held or are under attack:

> Men who would lose all patience, if we question'd their owning the sufficiency of scripture, and who have very much in their mouths a noisy out-cry, that the bible, the bible, is the religion of Protestants, have brought the charge of nonsense and contradiction against the great Protestant doctrines of the ever-blessed Trinity in Unity, absolute election, original sin, the necessity of an infinite satisfaction, the fullness and particularity of redemption, justification by the imputed righteousness of Christ, the inability of man to convert himself, the efficacy of divine grace, the perseverance of the saints, the resurrection of the same numerical body, and the eternity of hell torments: all these doctrines have been misrepresented, exploded, derided, and burlesqued by such as profess themselves Christians, nay, by such as would appear zealous to promote practical religion: so that the Deists have little to do, but to stand still and smile, whilst others were doing their work for them.[19]

These doctrines come together into the protestant soteriology that would have been familiar to the Founders. They emphasize the nature of God and his response to sin, the role of Christ, and the ultimate goal of displaying the glory of God. Taylor states it this way:

> However, this we must tenaciously adhere to, that it is inconsistent with the nature of God, for him to injure any of his perfections, to save such as deserve not his favour; we are not to doubt but that God will glorify one attribute as well as another, in rescuing ruin'd criminals: so that, he never would, in order to shew his sovereignty, or make known his mercy, suffer his justice to remain unsatisfied, and consequently not glorified, or his holiness and truth to be tarnish'd; but he is as much concerned to glorify his justice, and to shew forth his holiness and truth, as he can be to manifest his sovereignty, or to magnify his mercy.

The need for salvation is set in the context of God as both just and merciful. However redemption is achieved, it must be done in a way that affirms both of these aspects of God's nature. Taylor says:

> God therefore shew'd the greatness of his wisdom in contriving the method of man's salvation, that it might display Christ's satisfying for sin: in this way all his perfections are felt in the most amiable light, justice is glorified to the utmost, and has vindicated its rights, in that a satisfaction of infinite value has been yielded by an almighty Redeemer; holiness sparkles with the brightest lustre, seeing he, who is purity itself, has shew'd his hatred of sin to be so great, that he spared not his own Son, when he only knew sin by imputation; the truth of him, who is invariable in faithfulness, is fully established, in that he has exacted the punishment threaten'd; goodness appears in its full beauty, as a Redeemer is provided for such as have destroy'd themselves, and the greatest blessings are bestow'd freely upon the unworthy; mercy is display'd to the utmost, because provision is made for bringing sinners to partake of the happiness they had forfeited; wisdom and power are greatly magnified, since a way is laid out and finish'd, in which justice and holiness might not be injured, and yet grace and mercy might be eminently exalted.[20]

In the end, Taylor brings together special revelation and reason by claiming that this account of redemption is the most rational account:

> This method of man's salvation, which the scriptures teach, and as it is the only way of thinking which men can fall into, in order to glorify all God's perfections, it must be concluded to be the most

> rational scheme in the world. The design of God was to glorify his own perfections, to exalt Christ, to stain the pride of man's glory, and to shew the necessity of holiness; therefore, as the holy scripture declares and reveals this wonderful plan, it is no marvel that it should be ridiculed, as a huddle of foolish opinions, by the vain and proud pretenders of reason.[21]

THOMAS JEFFERSON

By way of contrast to Taylor, we will consider Thomas Jefferson and Thomas Paine. Jefferson rewrote the New Testament to exclude any supernatural or miraculous events, and Paine championed what he called natural religion and very explicitly rejected the Bible. Paine argued that the Bible gets in the way of true belief in God. We are going to turn from Taylor's perspective about the reasonableness of faith to the person most known at the time for attacking Christianity. Thomas Paine advocated what he called "common sense" in his arguments in favor of revolution. But in his book *The Age of Reason*, he gives us arguments against Christianity that are still popular today.

Although Thomas Jefferson was the primary author of the Declaration of Independence, he did not understand "creator" in the sense of Christianity. For Jefferson, God was understood in the sense of Deism or a kind of Unitarianism. He believed that most of the content of scripture had a corrupting influence by teaching people to be superstitions. He was one of the first modern biblical critics who sought to find the "historical Jesus" while extracting "moral teachings" from the Gospels. He put these together into what came to be known as the Jefferson Bible.

In taking this view, he was explicitly rejecting not only the doctrines of the Trinity and Incarnation but also vicarious atonement and the need for redemption through the death of Christ. He was rejecting the representative role of Adam and the representative role of Christ. However, he did not write directly on these matters in the way that Thomas Paine did. Paine's rejection is more explicit and contains in one form or another almost all of the criticisms from naturalism and biblical criticism that have been aimed at Christianity in the succeeding centuries.

Thomas Jefferson gives us a look at his theory of knowledge in *A Bill for Establishing Religious Freedom* drafted in 1777. First is that people cannot believe whatever they want but that their opinions are shaped by the evidence presented to their minds.[22] This means that there is a sense in which our beliefs are involuntary. And yet he says, second, that God has created the human mind free, that it has a freedom that cannot be taken away.[23] People can refuse to change their beliefs even to the point of death. In a way, these two propositions are in tension. I involuntarily believe what I do because of the evidence that is proposed to my mind. However, I am free to believe this. The resolution to the apparent tension is in my freedom to consider and pursue evidence and in my freedom to believe what I do apart from what others tell me to believe. Indeed, he says:

> That all attempts to influence it by temporal punishments, or burthens, or by civil incapacitations, tend only to beget habits of hypocrisy and meanness, and are a departure from the plan of the holy author of our religion, who being lord both of body and mind, yet chose not to propagate it by coercions on either, as was in his Almighty power to do, but to extend it by its influence on reason alone.[24]

He then condemns those who would take it upon themselves to tell others what to believe. All humans are fallible and uninspired, and so no one can claim authority over anyone else:

> That the impious presumption of legislators and rulers, civil as well as ecclesiastical, who, being themselves but fallible and uninspired men, have assumed dominion over the faith of others, setting up their own opinions and modes of thinking as the only true and infallible, and as such endeavoring to impose them on others, hath established and maintained false religions over the greatest part of the world and through all time.[25]

To compel anyone to give money for the advancement of beliefs he does not agree with or to support a teacher with whom he disagrees is an example of attacking this freedom, and Jefferson's identification of this problem foreshadows many early court cases in America.[26]

Next, Jefferson argues that there is no relationship between the civil realm or civil rights and believing a specific religious doctrine. He says:

> That our civil rights have no dependence on our religious opinions, any more than our opinions in physics or geometry; that therefore the proscribing any citizen as unworthy of the public confidence by laying upon him an incapacity of being called to offices of trust and emolument, unless he profess or renounce this or that religious opinion, is depriving him injuriously of those privileges and advantages to which, in common with his fellow citizens, he has a natural right; that it tends also to corrupt the principles of that very religion it is meant to encourage, by bribing, with a monopoly of worldly honours and emoluments, those who will externally profess and conform to it; that though indeed these are criminal who do not withstand such temptation, yet neither are those innocent who lay the bait in their way.[27]

Here, Jefferson must mean what he considers to be less basic religious beliefs. Otherwise, his assertion in the preceding quote is in tension with the Declaration of Independence, which claims that some self-evident truths are necessary for civil life together. It is this belief, this separation of religion from the rest of life, that will be an important component of the rest of American life and figure prominently in American law. Religious beliefs are taken to be irrelevant and, therefore, benign to social life, and law only factors into the equation when beliefs begin to disturb society.

> That it is time enough for the rightful purposes of civil government for its officers to interfere when principles break out into overt acts against peace and good order; and finally, that truth is great and will prevail if left to herself; that she is the proper and sufficient antagonist to error, and has nothing to fear from the conflict unless by human interposition disarmed of her natural weapons, free argument and debate; errors ceasing to be dangerous when it is permitted freely to contradict them.[28]

This idea of protecting the peace and good order of society will be quoted in later court decisions. The question is what beliefs exactly are *religious* and what beliefs are necessary for the foundation of a society? Is the belief that God exists religious and the belief that God does not exist not religious? Defining what counts as religion and a religious belief will be an important task for the Supreme Court if it is able to make rulings about religion.

Thomas Jefferson's own thinking about religion and the public sphere is grounded in his beliefs about human nature and God. On the one hand he speaks highly of the role of reason in coming to agreement about the truth. On the other he denies that humans are lost in sin and in need of redemption. Abraham Taylor, quoted earlier in the chapter, argued that reason teaches us both of these. Although Thomas Jefferson spoke highly of reason, we are left asking if he used reason fully or only partially in considering the human condition and in knowing God.

THOMAS PAINE

During the Great Awakening, some revivalists had called into question whether ministers who resisted them were Christians at all. This anticlerical attitude is evident in Thomas Paine, who saw no reason for attending church. He said, "My own mind is my own church. All national institutions of churches, whether Jewish, Christian, or Turkish, appear to me no other than human inventions set up to terrify and enslave mankind, and monopolize power and profit."[29]

Nor did he see any need for scripture. He argued that if there is special revelation, it is communicated directly from God to a prophet and that for the rest of us, we have no reason to believe the prophet's claims to have received such a communication. It becomes hearsay, and no one is obliged to believe it. "When Moses told the children of Israel that he received the two tables of the commandments from the hand of God, they were not obliged to believe him, because they had no other authority for it than his telling them so."[30]

Furthermore, he says that all of the supposed miracles that are cited to make Christianity unique and to authenticate its message were copied from the surrounding heathen religions. "Almost all the extraordinary men that lived under the heathen mythology were reputed to be the sons of some of their gods."[31] He reduces the entire Christian message to a copy of this heathen mythology:

> It is curious to observe how the theory of what is called the Christian Church, sprung out of the tail of the heathen mythology. A direct incorporation took place in the first instance, by making

> the reputed founder to be celestially begotten. The trinity of gods that then followed was no other than a reduction of the former plurality, which was about twenty or thirty thousand. The statue of Mary succeeded the statue of Diana of Ephesus. The deification of heroes changed into the canonization of saints. The Mythologists had gods for everything; the Christian Mythologists had saints for everything. The church became as crouded with the one, as the pantheon had been with the other; and Rome was the place of both. The Christian theory is little else than the idolatry of the ancient mythologists, accommodated to the purposes of power and revenue; and it yet remains to reason and philosophy to abolish the fraud.[32]

Nevertheless, Paine holds Jesus in some regard as a moral teacher. He distances Jesus from the rest of the New Testament and refers to him as a virtuous and amiable man. "Jesus practiced and preached benevolence and a similar system of morality that had been held by some Greek philosophers and was currently held by the Quakers."[33] As a moral system, Paine thinks it is of the highest standard and has not been surpassed by anyone.

One of the standards that Paine sets for religious belief is that if it is to be believed by all, then it must have proof and evidence that all should accept. He does not believe that the resurrection and ascension of Christ have any such proof. Even if they did occur, only those who saw would have the necessary proof to believe. For the rest of us, it is hearsay.

His standard for universal proof in support of what must be universally believed is important. However, his standard for what counts as proof is limited to empiricism. By *proof*, he seems to mean, in almost every case, either personal experience or consistency with common sense (what a person already believes). Because of this, he says of the Christian Gospel: "it is impossible to conceive a story more derogatory to the Almighty, more inconsistent with his wisdom, more contradictory to his power, than this story is."[34]

He continues from there to reject the entire Bible as filled with corruption and violence:

> Whenever we read the obscene stories, the voluptuous debaucheries, the cruel and torturous executions, the unrelenting vindictiveness,

> with which more than half the Bible is filled, it would be more consistent that we called it the word of a demon, than the Word of God. It is a history of wickedness, that has served to corrupt and brutalize mankind; and, for my own part, I sincerely detest it, as I detest everything that is cruel.[35]

Next he rejects the idea that there can be a written Word of God, since the Word must be unchangeable and human language is always in a state of change:

> If we permit ourselves to conceive right ideas of things, we must necessarily affix the idea, not only of unchangeableness, but of the utter impossibility of any change taking place, by any means or accident whatever, in that which we would honour with the name of the Word of God; and therefore the Word of God cannot exist in any written or human language.[36]

Paine relies on his empiricism, which is accompanied by a kind of literalism, to criticize the account of the Fall, original sin, imputation of sin to Christ, and the promise of life. He argues that these doctrines are based on ambiguities in meaning such as "death." Christ cannot have saved us from physical death, since we all still die. Therefore, it must be some kind of spiritual death, which Paine dismisses as a shift in meaning of the term. The idea that one person can represent others, whether it is Adam or Christ, is to Paine a quibble. He says:

> The declaratory sentence which, they say, was passed upon Adam, in case he ate of the apple, was not, that thou shalt surely be crucified, but, thou shalt surely die. The sentence was death, and not the manner of dying. Crucifixion, therefore, or any other particular manner of dying, made no part of the sentence that Adam was to suffer, and consequently, even upon their own tactic, it could make no part of the sentence that Christ was to suffer in the place of Adam. A fever would have done as well as a cross, if there was any occasion for either.

Paine recognizes that the teaching about Christ's atoning work is related to the teaching that Adam was created without death. Death was imposed later. Paine also recognizes that the term "death" can be ambiguous. He thinks it either means physical death or future damnation. Working from this premise he rejects the doctrines of representation, imputation, and substitution in the following way:

> This sentence of death, which, they tell us, was thus passed upon Adam, must either have meant dying naturally, that is, ceasing to live, or have meant what these mythologists call damnation; and consequently, the act of dying on the part of Jesus Christ, must, according to their system, apply as a prevention to one or other of these two things happening to Adam and to us. That it does not prevent our dying is evident, because we all die; and if their accounts of longevity be true, men die faster since the crucifixion than before: and with respect to the second explanation, (including with it the natural death of Jesus Christ as a substitute for the eternal death or damnation of all mankind), it is impertinently representing the Creator as revoking the sentence, by a pun or a quibble upon the word death. That manufacturer of quibbles, St. Paul, if he wrote the books that bear his name, has helped this quibble on by making another quibble upon the word Adam. He makes there to be two Adams; the one who sins in fact, and suffers by proxy; the other who sins by proxy, and suffers in fact. A religion thus interlarded with quibble, subterfuge, and pun, has a tendency to instruct its professors in the practice of these arts. They acquire the habit without being aware of the cause.[37]

He continues to reject the idea of imputation and representation. He says that in no system of justice would it be acceptable for an innocent party to pay the penalty for a guilty party. Justice requires that the guilty party is the one who pays the penalty.

> But if I have committed a crime, every circumstance of the case is changed. Moral justice cannot take the innocent for the guilty even if the innocent would offer itself. To suppose justice to do this, is to destroy the principle of its existence, which is the thing itself. It is then no longer justice. It is indiscriminate revenge.[38]

His conclusion from this is that there is no such thing as redemption.

> And that, in truth, there is no such thing as redemption; that it is fabulous; and that man stands in the same relative condition with his Maker he ever did stand, since man existed; and that it is his greatest consolation to think so.[39]

By way of contrast with the scriptures that he rejects, Paine argues that the works of nature are the universal revelation of God to all humans.

These make God known to all nations, whereas Jesus could never have done so, being isolated to one small part of the world.

> It is only in the creation that all our ideas and conceptions of a word of God can unite. The Creation speaketh an universal language, independently of human speech or human language, multiplied and various as they be. It is an ever existing original, which every man can read. It cannot be forged; it cannot be counterfeited; it cannot be lost; it cannot be altered; it cannot be suppressed. It does not depend upon the will of man whether it shall be published or not; it publishes itself from one end of the earth to the other. It preaches to all nations and to all worlds; and this word of God reveals to man all that is necessary for man to know of God.[40]

On the one hand Paine affirms that general revelation reveals God, while on the other he denies that it reveals the reality of sin and the need for redemption. Paine relies on a combination of the teleological and cosmological arguments to support his belief in God. Time cannot have had an infinite duration and, therefore, must have had a beginning. This first cause of creation is God. Furthermore, the world around us testifies to the existence of God. He maintains that we can know very little about God. Therefore, what general revelation does reveal about God is bare and not full.

> The only idea man can affix to the name of God, is that of a first cause, the cause of all things. And, incomprehensibly difficult as it is for a man to conceive what a first cause is, he arrives at the belief of it, from the tenfold greater difficulty of disbelieving it. It is difficult beyond description to conceive that space can have no end; but it is more difficult to conceive an end. It is difficult beyond the power of man to conceive an eternal duration of what we call time; but it is more impossible to conceive a time when there shall be no time. In like manner of reasoning, everything we behold carries in itself the internal evidence that it did not make itself.[41]

And:

> First, Canst thou by searching find out God? Yes. Because, in the first place, I know I did not make myself, and yet I have existence; and by searching into the nature of other things, I find that no other thing could make itself; and yet millions of other things exist; therefore it is, that I know, by positive conclusion resulting from

> this search, that there is a power superior to all those things, and that power is God.[42]

Whereas Paine affirms the revelation of God's existence and nature from general revelation, this revelation is minimal, and he rejects the idea that humans need redemption. And yet it is undeniable that humans have not seen this revelation from general revelation. This revelation has been rejected and replaced with idolatry. This is the condition that raises the question of redemption. If humans have rejected what God has made known from general revelation, then the question is how will God redeem them from this culpable ignorance? This is the subject of special revelation, and yet Paine rejects its contents. Like Jefferson, Paine spoke highly of reason and yet did not use reason fully to critically examine his own assumptions about knowledge, God, and the human condition.

CONCLUSION

Although Paine relied on teleological and cosmological arguments to prove God's existence, these same arguments were rejected, in the name of reason, by philosophers in the nineteenth century. The implication is that Paine relied on what he called common sense and reason to reject the doctrines of scripture and redemption. Later thinkers will also appeal to common sense and reason to reject what Paine thought he had proven about God. Paine left room for the God of deism, and in this sense his beliefs are consistent with the Declaration of Independence. But he did not successfully prove his beliefs and so it is not surprising that later generations rejected his deism while amplifying his criticisms of Christianity.

The challenge is: Why do we need even the God of Thomas Paine? What if reason and evidence can be used by the materialists or pantheists to show that there is no such God? Isn't a person living in the age of reason required to follow that evidence? The century after Thomas Paine and the Declaration of Independence was one of increased tension between belief in God and the supposed requirements of reason. By the end of that century, the relationship to God and law is ambiguous at best. If the law guides public life together, and is therefore closely connected to reason, and belief in God is a purely private matter, then the argument is that belief in God should not influence law or public life. "God" no longer need refer to the creator but could have a number of different definitions.

2 THE REFORMED INFLUENCE ON COMMON SENSE PHILOSOPHY

In many instances, religious persons refer to the Declaration of Independence in order to support the claim that America is a Christian nation. This is an ambiguous claim. It could mean that most of the persons living in the United States throughout its history have identified as Christians belonging to one denomination or another. Or it could mean that the philosophical assumptions behind the political theory of the United States are grounded in Christianity. In response to this, the theologian Martin E. Marty says that the ideas of the rule of law, a representative republic, and limited powers of branches of government could have emerged in non-Christian religious contexts. Instead of arguing about whether this is a Christian nation, he says, "They will do better and serve better if they are content with interpreting and acting in a nation that lacks precise or detailed religious definition. This calls for citizens to make decisions on relevant subjects despite some blurring of the lines that distinguish what is represented by the terms 'church and state.'"[1]

Indeed, the terms "religion" and "church" have been and continue to be ambiguous. He sees the original intent of disestablishment as "The original goal was to respect consciences and protect liberties while they were still pursuing the common good."[2] If this is true, then the idea of the common good is distinct from particular religious beliefs. The term "religion" in U.S. history has often referred to organized institutions that teach about morality and the afterlife. By way of contrast, the common good is about the goods of this life that all persons regardless of religious affiliation can pursue together. This division of religion and "the present life" has led to an increased seclusion of religion into the private realm. This division is supported by the idea that we cannot really know what is the highest good or what is the moral law that teaches how to achieve that good. Therefore, all opinions in these matters are equally treated as mere opinions. Similarly, we cannot know if there is an afterlife or what it entails, and so beliefs about this are mere opinion and private. But we can know what are the common goods of this life, and it is on the basis of this knowledge that public decisions can be made.

The essence of this is in skepticism about religious claims. Knowledge has authority, but mere opinion cannot have public authority. This is consistent with the relationship we have seen among epistemology, metaphysics, and ethics. A problem that will continue to present itself in our study is "how can we know what are common goods if we cannot know what is the highest good?" And "how can we know what are common goods if we cannot know what is real and what is only temporary and grounded in appearances?"

It is worth noting that the Northwest Ordinance (1789), in the 1st Statute articles 1 and 2, says, "No person, demeaning himself in a peaceful and orderly manner, shall ever be molested on account of his mode of worship or religious sentiments, in the said territory" and "Religion, morality, and knowledge, being necessary to good government and the happiness of mankind, schools and the means of education shall forever be encouraged."[3] This ordinance covered the lands from the Appalachian Mountains, between Canada and the Great Lakes in the north and the Ohio River and Mississippi River to the south and west. This area, especially Ohio, later became an important part of the Second Great Awakening and missionary efforts by the Protestant denominations.

In keeping with these sentiments, in 1819, Congress and President James Monroe passed an act that appropriated $10,000 to employ "'capable persons of good moral character' to instruct the Indians."[4] This resulted in a Supreme Court case when one such missionary was charged with residing in the Cherokee nation without permission. Chief Justice Marshall gave the opinion that since "he was seized, while performing, under the sanction of the chief magistrate of the Union, those duties which the humane policy adopted by Congress had recommended,"[5] the penalty of the lower court must be overturned.

Massachusetts saw a large number of cases involving state aid or sanction of ministers. This was true in the case of state aid to Harvard. But it became especially divisive in the case of ministers and parishioners who disagreed about Trinitarian and Unitarian doctrine. A number of instances occurred when Unitarian ministers were installed in Congregationalist churches but were rejected by the parishioners. These cases made their way to the Massachusetts Supreme Court with justices that were Unitarians. "Between 1820 and 1834 nearly one hundred Congregationalist parishes fell under Unitarian control – over one-quarter of the Congregationalist parishes in the commonwealth… The Trinitarians estimated that Unitarians took $608,000 worth of property."[6]

These cases were decided in light of Article III of the state constitution. It read:

> As the happiness of a people and the good order and preservation of civil government essentially depend upon piety, religion, and morality, and as these cannot be generally diffused through a community but by the institution of the public worship of God and of the public instructions in piety, religion and morality: Therefore, To promote their happiness and to secure the good order and preservation of their government, the people of this Commonwealth have a right to invest their legislature with the power to authorize and require, and the legislature shall, from time to time, authorize and require, the several towns, parishes, precincts, and other bodies-politic or religious societies to make suitable provision, at their own expense, for the institution of the public worship of God and for the support and maintenance of public Protestant teachers of piety, religion, and morality … That the several towns, parishes, precincts, and other bodies-politic, or religious societies shall at all times have the exclusive right of electing their public teachers and of contracting with them for their support and maintenance.[7]

In the case *Barnes v. First Parish in Falmouth*, the court said, "The object of a free civil government is the promotion and happiness of its citizens. These effects cannot be produced, but by the knowledge and practice of our moral duties, which comprehend all the social and civil obligations of man to man, and of citizens to the state."[8] In elaborating on this, it was further said,

> Christianity has the promise not only of this, but of a future life, it cannot be denied that public instruction in piety, religion, and morality, by Protestant teachers, may have beneficial effect beyond the present state of existence. And the people are to be applauded, as well for their benevolence as for their wisdom, that, in selecting a religion whose precepts and sanctions might supply the defects in civil government, necessarily limited in its power, and supported only by temporal penalties, they adopted a religion founded in truth.[9]

The parish tax could be directed by the individual to support the teacher with whom there was agreement. In this matter of Trinitarians and Unitarians, the court seemed to see no difference in terms of the goals stated above of service of religion to the state. The truth of the matter regarding those doctrines was not related to the goods of religion in society. This is a kind of skepticism about what can be known and about how it relates to law and the good life.

Even so, in *Baker v. Fales* (1820), Chief Justice Parker decided in favor of a Unitarian minister who had been rejected by the congregation. Since many who rejected him had left the church, and new deacons had been put in place, the justice maintained that the church's constitution had been followed in keeping the minister. He said:

> The authority of the church should be of that invisible, but powerful nature, which results from superior gravity, piety, and devout example. It will then have its proper effect upon the congregation, who will cheerfully yield to the wishes of those who are best qualified to select the candidate ... The condition of the members of a church is thought to be hard, where the minister elected by the parish is not approved by them ... in the present state of our laws, and as they are likely to continue, there is no hardship, although there may be some inconvenience; for dissenting members of the church, the parish, may join any other church and society, or they may institute a new society... It is true, if there are any parish funds, they will lose the benefit of them by removal; but an inconvenience of this sort will never be felt, when a case of conscience is in question.[10]

Although the justice in this case wished to stay out of questions of theology and instead to appear as only involved in a matter of property, the result had theological assumptions. The idea that religion was a benefit to society and should be supported but that theological differences between Unitarians and Trinitarians were benign to that benefit is itself a theological position. What we can see from these cases was that Christians were in a state of division. They were not able to agree and build together in unity. The consequence was that their divisions spilled over into the civil courts and into life more generally. To deal with these divisions would require either getting involved in settling the truth of the matter about the nature of God or in declaring that these differences were unimportant to the role that religion played in society. The latter course is the one that was taken. It was a course that was grounded in skepticism about theological matters while also affirming some beneficial role for some religious beliefs such as in an ambiguous "God" and a future life. However, the benefit of even these beliefs would be challenged.

THE ENGLISH REFORMATION

During the English Civil War in the mid-seventeenth century, the Westminster Assembly was called to order with the purpose of drafting a doctrinal statement for the church. It included representatives from the Presbyterians, Anglicans, and reformed theologians from the Continent. It produced the Westminster Confession and the Westminster Shorter and Larger Catechism. Upon its completion in 1648, it was immediately requested by Congregationalist ministers in New England and has continued to have an authoritative role in Presbyterian churches in the United States. Whether a minister affirms the doctrines in the Confession has been a point of contention in church trials in the U.S. over the past centuries. These often involved questions about the sovereignty of God in salvation and the inspired and infallible nature of the scriptures.

However, the Confession begins with epistemology before moving on to metaphysics and ethics. It does this by affirming that the goodness, wisdom, and power of God are known by reason and through the works of creation and providence. However, because of sin, which is the rejection of this knowledge of God, there is a need for redemption, and the knowledge of redemption is available only through the scriptures of the Old and New Testaments.

From here, it affirms the nature of God as creator and ruler, the role of Christ as the only mediator between God and man[,] and the vicarious atonement for sin. It also affirms as the chief end of man, or highest good, the knowledge of the glory of God. The Larger and Shorter Catechism argue that the Ten Commandments are a summary of the natural moral law and contain the duty required by God for humans to attain the highest good of knowing the glory of God. It contains what might be called the doxological focus of life: that all of life is aimed at the knowledge of the glory of God.

Because this was a foundational document for American Presbyterians, and because of their role in educational institutions like Princeton and Princeton Seminary, it has had an impact on American thinking about religion and the state. It gives a much fuller account of the epistemology, metaphysics, and ethics than does the Declaration of Independence. And yet it affirms that the good and God can be known by all persons from the "light of nature." As a statement of faith, it represents the output of the best minds of the English Christian world at the end of the Reformation, summarizing the teachings of the Reformation after much discussion.

CHALLENGES TO THE REFORMATION IN AMERICA

However, in American history, it has been challenged from secular sources as well as from Christian sources. The secular challenges are generally aimed at the nature of God (a move from theism to pantheism and process theology), the nature of man (as evolved and not directly created by God), the source of knowledge (intuitions leading to pantheism), the inspiration of scripture (as just another human construct among many), and the good (man in the image of the animal, or man as divine and part of God). The Christian challenges are from sources that reject the sovereignty of God. Revivalism from the Second Great Awakening onward insisted on the sovereignty of man in accepting salvation and viewed this as part of an individualism that fit into the American dream. Similarly, the intuition that freedom and predestination were at odds led to affirming individual freedom at the cost of predestination and God's sovereignty. We will consider the most notable figure in this area, Charles Finney, who dismissed the Westminster Confession as a "paper pope." Although ordained as a Presbyterian, he admitted at his ordination to having never read the Confession.

These challenges from Finney indicate a shift in epistemology, metaphysics, and ethics. He relied on a kind of intuition to affirm the truth of Christianity. His view of God is less than theism, and his view of the human will is more than a created being. He taught that the highest good is achieved in the afterlife in heaven, in contrast to the knowledge of God, which is available both now and in the afterlife.

These challenges were not limited to the nineteenth century, although we will spend time looking at that period. They date back to Hobbes, Locke, and Grotius, who framed political theories that challenged the ideas of the Reformation. One of these supposed challenges is that humans can know about the good and law by reason. As we saw, this is affirmed in the Westminster Confession. However, some branches of Christianity insisted that all knowledge is only from the scriptures.

Another challenge was to the providence of God and the purpose of human life. It became common and remains so today to identify the good with happiness. Moral and political theories used happiness as the standard for assessing what ought to be done and how to arrange society. The problem with this is that what makes persons happy depends on what they believe is good. The implication is that the good cannot be known, and instead, society is arranged to permit as much freedom about what is good as possible so that people can achieve happiness, even if it is only temporary because it is grounded in a false view of what is good.

Furthermore, these philosophers spoke about a "state of nature" out of which human society emerged. They sometimes would refer to the Biblical narrative, but it played no real role in their thinking. Their "state of nature" foreshadows Darwin's account of evolution and the ascent of man. Rather than having been given by God the command to be fruitful and multiply and have dominion over the earth, and with a covenant between God and the first man as a covenant of works followed by a covenant of grace, humans in the "state of nature" find themselves in competition with all other humans and only relating to God, if at all, on an individual level. The state is formed to protect individual interests from what Hobbes called the "war of all against all."

Finally, in this perspective, although humans can act in ways that are morally wrong, they are not "fallen." This is an early rejection of Christian theology that led to the rejection of the doctrine of Christ and his atoning work that we saw in Jefferson and Paine. In this view, humans are essentially good, and their pursuit of individual happiness is in accord with the larger social welfare. The state is needed to help organize this and protect freedom but not primarily because humans are fallen and in need of limitations on their propensities.

We can see some of this change in American Christians even in the First Great Awakening and the decades after it leading up to the American Revolution. Rather than speaking about man's chief end or highest good as the knowledge of the glory of God, Jonathan Edwards spoke of it as disinterested benevolence for all being. There was an anti-intellectual, or perhaps better a noncognitivist, strain in Edwards that made experience the epistemological absolute. In putting religious experience in such a role, he set up the thinkers we will consider later like Finney, Emerson, Darwin, and Tillich to make claims from their experience that increasingly moved away from Christianity. Clearly, this was not Edwards's intent. However, because of his epistemology and his belief about the good, he introduced a shift in focus that reverberates to the present.

The problem that was missed is that experience must be interpreted; no experience is self-verifying or self-interpreting. People who have the same experience can disagree about what it means and how it is to be understood. Thus, experience itself (while a component of knowledge) is not the highest authority but must be interpreted by reason as the laws of thought for coherence and consistency. Indeed, each individual does interpret his/her experiences but often without recognizing that this is occurring.

The First Great Awakening produced a dichotomy in American thinking about religion and the good society that continues to this day. It can be fit into the Hegelian theory of history as a thesis and antithesis. However, to date, it has not produced a synthesis. Instead, I think it reveals what I have called elsewhere a reverse Hegelian dialectic. That is, the dichotomy gives us two sides of the same coin that share presuppositions that need to be brought to light and critically examined. The impasse is only present because of these presuppositions.

In the First Great Awakening, the tension arose between what came to be called the Old Side/Old Light and New Side/New Light among the Congregationalists and Presbyterians. The Old Side/Old Light viewed the revival with suspicion and affirmed the need for preparation to receive the Gospel. As such, they were called Preparationists. In a way, they were the conservative and traditional side of the debate. The New Side/New Light view the revival as the working of the Holy Spirit to regenerate unbelievers and [viewed] opposition to this work as evidence of unbelief. At best, the Preparationists were too formalistic; at worst, they were directly opposing the work of God. This led figures like George Whitfield to question if such ministers were even Christians. Whereas the Old Side/Old Light continued to think of the highest good in terms of the glory of God, this was often understood to mean the enjoyment of God in heaven. The New Side/New Light also emphasized heaven but included disinterested benevolence for all being. We can see these two views of the good even in our own day in competing political theories about how to construct a good society.

This dichotomy continued in the Second Great Awakening between the Old School and New School. It can be seen in the other revivals down to the present day under Moody, Billy Sunday, and Billy Graham. It can be seen in continued conflict at the political level between those who emphasize the conservation of tradition and those who emphasize individual experience and intuition. It is in essence a tension of epistemology between tradition and experience/intuition arising out of competing beliefs about the nature of humanity and the highest good.

WARS OF RELIGION

The philosophy and political theory of the Declaration of Independence are firmly rooted in the Enlightenment, which in turn was a response to the European Wars of Religion. The Americans were especially (but not exclusively) influenced by the Scottish Enlightenment and its emphasis on common sense and first principles. This can be seen in its affirming that some things are self-evident in that these are the place to start. What happens when society no longer holds to Enlightenment principles or the idea that there are things that are self-evident? Or what if there is disagreement about what is self-evident?

We are going to look at some of the ideas from the Scottish Enlightenment that influenced commonsense thinking. These were a response to skepticism. David Hume, one of the British empiricists, drew out the implications of empiricism that led him to show how it leads to skepticism. Other Scottish philosophers like Thomas Reid tried to respond to this skepticism to show how knowledge is possible. Skepticism says knowledge is not possible, and there are only opinions. Reid thought that there are some first principles that all humans believe, and from these we can establish knowledge. These first principles were in various areas of life, including mathematics and metaphysics but also morality. In the area of morality he argued that there are obligations that are commonsense ideas that all people have.

These first principles are necessary to affirm if there is going to be dialogue, and for anyone who does not affirm them, there is no need to continue discussion. Discussion with the person who does not agree to these cannot go anywhere and cannot result in an agreement or clarification. All people in some sense agree even if they are not aware of it. This can be understood to say that all people presuppose these first principles as the necessary conditions for knowledge. These first principles are taken for granted and rarely thought about. Now the first principles that Reid identified are not at all like the ones that the Declaration of Independence begins with.

The Wars of Religion were devastating in their impact. They seemed to indicate that knowledge is not possible from scripture or the church. The historical and philosophical background of the American Revolution and its thinking about religion and the state are the Wars of Religion. The wars were part of the structure of the church-state relationship. The structure of the state's authority and laws rested on theological and philosophical assumptions that were challenged by the Reformation. This has been analyzed from different perspectives such as individualism, the personal conscience, the rise of democracy, and changes in the market economy.

However, behind each of these are ideas about the nature of God, knowledge, and law. At a basic level, the Reformation challenged the authority of supposed knowledge. Authority shifted to the text of the Scriptures in matters of redemption and salvation. This was a reformation rather than a revolution in the sense that it was a return to the scriptures as the basis for authority and knowledge. The Reformation developed space within which thinkers were able to work and question prior assumptions, especially from Aristotle, that had become embedded in theology and philosophy. Presupposed in the well-known theological disputes between Roman Catholics and Protestants were two different ideas about how knowledge is attained and the ultimate source of authority.

The implications about law and government would require changes. When each of these changes was resisted, the Wars of Religion resulted. The intellectual response to these wars of religion was to look for what is universal in all humans. Fighting about competing interpretations of scripture was set aside as insufficient as a basis for authority and law. This era is called the Enlightenment, self-described, because its philosophers viewed themselves as going beyond partisan divisions and looking for what can be known by all persons through general revelation. It was a search for what is common to all, in contrast to scriptures and religion, which were understood to be personal and divisive. The question became how to contain these divisions while searching for what is universal.

The British empiricists like John Locke found both the foundation and the universal starting point in the senses. This fit together well with the new science of Isaac Newton as well as the new political science that was being developed by thinkers like Thomas Hobbes and Hugo Grotius. It also set a limit on theological claims. Beliefs about special revelation in miracles began to be isolated to the private arena of life and had no authority in a public area of life because they cannot be confirmed by what is common to all. People would inevitably have beliefs and commitments about things like miracles, but these commitments had to be contained in a way that did not divide society and result in wars as they had in the sixteenth and seventeenth centuries.

Although the Enlightenment made noble claims about knowledge and what can be known by all, it also contained a latent skepticism that was never resolved. This skepticism showed itself in many forms, including the critique of David Hume and of foundationalism itself. The Empiricists looked for the foundation, or starting point, for knowledge and, therefore, of authority. Formally speaking, every system does this; even those who claim to be antifoundationalist have an explanation of their starting point. By grounding knowledge in the senses, being the senses of the material world, Enlightenment thinkers believed they found a way to avoid allowing personal opinions to have final authority. In this theory, the senses can be double-checked by others, and the whole system can be turned into the scientific method. As Enlightenment thinkers learned more about the world's religions, belief in the Christian Scriptures appeared more and more arbitrary. The same could be said about the miracles of the Christian religion. These were all a matter of interpretation. They could not be confirmed through an objective process like a scientific method through which agreement could be attained.

We will look at these criticisms in the next chapter. Right now, we want to consider some of the foundational claims made by English Protestants that affected the American Revolution. These can be found as summarized in the Westminster Confession of Faith. In its own historical context, it was completed during the English Civil War and, with the restoration of a Catholic king, was in general set aside by the established Church of England. However, it continued to have influence on English and Scottish Presbyterians and in formulating both the Presbyterian and Congregationalist churches in America.

JAMES MADISON

In order to get a sense of how these general concerns were expressed in particular by American thinkers, we will use James Madison as a representative: specifically, his arguments in *The Federalist Papers* in support of the Constitution. While some persons note that the Constitution, unlike the Declaration of Independence, does not refer to God and so have called it a godless constitution, there are important principles in it that seem to be more akin to the Reformation's view of humanity than to the Enlightenment's view. Specifically, it has been observed that the limitations of powers within the government and the need for limitations in human life are due to the influence of the doctrine of the Fall.

Madison speaks about how knowledge begins with first principles or primary truths: "In disquitions of every kind, there are certain primary truths, or first principles, upon which all subsequent reasonings must depend. These contain an internal evidence which, antecedent to all reflection or combination, commands the assent of the mind."[11] He illustrates this from geometry and explains how these first principles cannot be denied:

> Of this nature are the maxims in geometry, that "the whole is greater than its part; things equal to the same are equal to one another; two straight lines cannot enclose a space; and all right angles are equal to each other." Of the same nature are these other maxims in ethics and politics, that there cannot be an effect without a cause; that the means ought to be proportioned to the end; that every power ought to be commensurate with its object; that there ought to be no limitation of a power destined to effect a purpose which is itself incapable of limitation. And there are other truths in the two latter sciences which, if they cannot pretend to rank in the class of axioms, are yet such direct inferences from them, and so obvious in themselves, and so agreeable to the natural and unsophisticated dictates of common-sense, that they challenge the assent of a sound and unbiased mind, with a degree of force and conviction almost equally irresistible.[12]

Anticipating the objection that morality and political theory are not like geometry, Madison explains why there is this appearance:

> Though it cannot be pretended that the principles of moral and political knowledge have, in general, the same degree of certainty with those of the mathematics, yet they have much better claims in this respect than, to judge from the conduct of men in particular situations, we should be disposed to allow them. The obscurity is much oftener in the passions and prejudices of the reasoner than in the subject. Men, upon too many occasions, do not give their own understandings fair play; but, yielding to some untoward bias, they entangle themselves in words and confound themselves in subtleties.[13]

The idea here is that the subjects themselves are clear and knowable but that there is something in the human that keeps him/her from knowing. If these passions and prejudices could be kept in check, then knowledge would be possible, and we would see that these fields of inquiry are as clear as is geometry. Madison believed that the Americans had a unique opportunity to do just this. In planning their union, they were addressing the question as to whether humans can decide on their own the important question of establishing a good government from reflection and choice or if instead humanity was always to depend on "accident and force" for its political constitutions.[14]

This might be called an Enlightenment view of human reason. But this is only in contrast to those who say that all knowledge is from the scripture and that unregenerate humans cannot know anything. As we saw earlier, the Westminster Catechisms affirmed that the light of nature teaches the fullness of the natural moral law and that the Ten Commandments are a summary of this. Similarly, the Confession taught that the light of nature teaches that there is a God and that the chief end of man, the highest good, is to know the glory of God.

What distinguishes Madison's thinking is, therefore, not Enlightenment versus Reformation but his view of knowledge and the good life. In response to the Wars of Religions, he says, "For in politics, as in religion, it is equally absurd to aim at making proselytes by fire and sword. Heresies in either can rarely be cured by persecution."[15] This affirms something about human nature and how beliefs are formed. On this basis, it also affirms something about the powers of government. It isn't that a government shouldn't attempt to make converts by the sword; it is rather that this does not work because it is contrary to the nature of belief formation.

In contrast to much of American eschatology – the theory of the end times – that we will see in the centuries after the Revolution, there was still at this time a kind of postmillennialism that affirmed that history progressed, albeit through trials, toward the victory of good over evil. This postmillennialism is interpreted in varying ways all depending on how the good is understood. Thus, it has incurred a bad reputation because some of its representatives in the nineteenth and early twentieth centuries identified "the good" with the increase of technology and overcoming of natural evils such as suffering, famine, and poverty. In contrast to this is amillennialism, which claims that divisions between good and evil persist until the end. We see a kind of secular account of this in Madison, who says of political theory:

> The science of politics, however, like most other sciences, has received great improvement. The efficacy of various principles is now well understood, which were either not known at all, or imperfectly known to the ancients. The regular distribution of power into distinct departments; the introduction of legislative balances and checks; the institution of courts composed of judges holding their offices during good behavior; the representation of the people in the legislature by deputies of their own election: these are wholly new discoveries, or have made their principal progress towards perfection in modern times.[16]

One of Madison's arguments in favor of the Constitution in *The Federalist Papers* is the ability of a Union to combat the powers of factions.[17] These include political factions but also religious factions. For Madison, this is about how to protect the public good: "that the public good is disregarded in the conflicts of rival parties, and that measures are too often decided, not according to the rules of justice and the rights of the minor party, but by the superior force of an interested and overbearing majority."[18]

By a faction, Madison means a group of citizens, either a majority or a minority, who are moved by a common attitude or passion or interest that is set in contrast to the rights of the other citizens or to the common good of the community.[19] In this sense, he seems to distinguish between what can be known about the common good and the foundational beliefs and values needed to support a government and the personal feelings or wants of a faction that are set in contrast to these. The question is what is included on each side, what things can be known, and what things are relegated to private passions and opinions. He says:

> As long as the reason of man continues fallible, and he is at liberty to exercise it, different opinions will be formed. As long as the connection subsists between his reason and his self-love, his opinions and his passions will have a reciprocal influence on each other; and the former will be objects to which the latter will attach themselves. The diversity in the faculties of men, from which the

> rights of property originate, is not less an insuperable obstacle to a uniformity of interests.[20]

Madison's description in this quote could refer to humans in their fallen condition, but it could also be a comment on the finitude of humans even though they are not fallen. Within each person is a conflict of interests, and this conflict flows over into a conflict with the common good of the public. This is a realist description of the human condition but does not explain why the human condition is that way or if it can be remedied. There is in this supposedly realist description a latent skepticism about the ability for humans to know the basic things. There is a kind of psychology of the human condition wherein beliefs about what is good are set against feelings and desires.

Although this is a common assessment of the relationship between beliefs and desires, it should not be taken as the correct interpretation of that relationship. There do often appear to be conflicts within each of us between what we believe we should do and what we desire to do. However, a further analysis can reveal that behind this conflict is a conflict of beliefs, not simply one of belief and desire. That conflict is between competing beliefs about what is good. Socrates gave perhaps the most well-known analysis of this in the *Meno*, where he argued that humans always desire, or choose to do, what they believe is good. The problem is, therefore, one of knowing what is actually good rather than what appears, mistakenly, to be good at a given moment. This analysis keeps the problem centered on knowing the good rather than allowing a person to say, "I know what is good but don't want the good." Such a claim quickly dissolves when the person is asked to prove what they claim to know: if you know what is good, then show that you know it. The claim quickly turns into "Well, I don't know the good, but I have an opinion about what is good." Socrates argues that we can have competing opinions about what is good within ourselves, but if we actually know, then we would be able to set aside false opinions and pursue what is actually good.

This applies to the issues that Madison is discussing because he is considering the reality of competing beliefs within a person and then within a society. His analysis of factions remains at the level of beliefs in conflict with passions rather than backing up to consider the beliefs presupposed in the passions. Of these, he says, "The latent causes of faction are thus sown in the nature of man; and we see them everywhere brought into different degrees of activity, according to the different circumstances of civil society. A zeal for different opinions concerning religion, concerning government, and many other points, as well of speculation as of practice."[21] Again, his description can be understood to be a realist account of the reality of human divisions. Humans have the ability and propensity to divide into fierce conflicts over almost any subject. What are otherwise frivolous and fanciful distinctions have engendered the most violent conflicts that can be imagined.[22]

Madison's analysis of this remains at the level of description, and he moves to give a solution that maintains these violent conflicts while combating their destructive influence. "The regulation of these various and interfering interests forms the principal task of modern legislation, and involves the spirit of party and faction in the necessary and ordinary operations of the government."[23] Given his belief that this is the constant and unchangeable condition of human nature, the only solution he considers but then rejects is that enlightened statesmen could work with these competing interests and make them subservient to the public good. This will not be a lasting solution, Madison says, because there will not always be enlightened statesmen at the helm.[24]

The only solution is to control the effects of these factions.[25] "Ambition must be made to counteract ambition."[26] Because of these considerations, he says:

> It may be a reflection on human nature, that such devices should be necessary to control the abuses of government. But what is government itself, but the greatest of all reflections on human nature? If men were angels, no government would be necessary. If angels were to govern men, neither external nor internal controls on government would be necessary. In framing a government which is to be administered by men over men, the great difficulty lies in this: you must first enable the government to control the governed; and in the next place oblige it to control itself. A dependence on the people is, no doubt, the primary control on the government; but experience has taught mankind the necessity of auxiliary precautions. This policy of supplying, by opposite and rival interests, the defect of better motives, might be traced through the whole system of human affairs, private as well as public.[27]

This solution is practical and is grounded in the experience of Europe as it came through the Wars of Religion. No solution was reached in those wars. The factions that existed at the beginning of that conflict continued to exist in Madison's time. This gives the appearance that there is no resolution of these kinds of divisions, and, therefore, the solution of how to live together must include calculating that these divisions will persist.

While it may be true that there are such divisions, it is not equally clear that they must persist. However, Madison is here setting the limits of a government that will rule over individuals and groups that are at odds over fundamental beliefs and desires. The question remains open as to whether this reality must persist. He seems to think it will when he says:

> Different interests necessarily exist in different classes of citizens. If a majority be united by a common interest, the rights of the minority will be insecure. There are but two methods of providing against this evil: the one by creating a will in the community independent of the majority – that is, of the society itself; the other, by comprehending in the society so many separate descriptions of citizens as will render an unjust combination of a majority of the whole very improbable, if not impracticable.[28]

Far from resolving these divisions, Madison finds security in allowing them to persist:

> Whilst all authority in it will be derived from and dependent on the society, the society itself will be broken into so many parts, interests, and classes of citizens, that the rights of individuals, or of the minority, will be in little danger from interested combinations of the majority. In a free government the security for civil rights must be the same as that for religious rights. It consists in the one case in the multiplicity of interests, and in the other in the multiplicity of sects.[29]

He believes that the alternative is "a society under the forms of which the stronger faction can readily unite and oppress the weaker, anarchy may as truly be said to reign as in a state of nature, where the weaker individual is not secured against the violence of the stronger."[30]

And so we see that from the beginning, the best minds arguing in favor of the Constitution understood that religious divisions, with the possibility of becoming passionate and violent, would continue in the republic. The method was to set up limitations on powers and to set such factions and their interests against each other so as to temper their ability to cause problems. If this is a realistic position about the existence of factions, it offers no solution about how humans can arrive at unity.

Out of this, one wonders what exactly can be known and what is a matter of opinion and will never be resolved. Madison recognizes that there are fundamental principles needed for the establishment and continuation of a republic. If this foundation cannot be known, then there can be no hope either of establishing or of continuing a constitutional republic. If the public good cannot be known, then there can be no hope of preserving it in contrast to the passions and desires of competing factions. Therefore, it must be assumed that the public good can be known and that foundational principles, perhaps those mentioned by Madison about the limits of government and human rights, can be known. But then the question is why these cannot be further applied and implications drawn out to resolve the conflicts between passions.

Either factions are about basic questions including those that are fundamental to a Union and Republic, or they are about secondary matters of taste not resolvable by drawing out the implication of basic questions. If the Union is to continue, then these factions must be of the second kind. However, what we see in the Wars of Religion and in the kinds of conflicts that have come up in American history is that factions are divisions about basic questions concerning the nature of knowledge, reality, and the good.

Thus, the ongoing tensions we will see between the law and religious freedom are nested in this original skepticism about the ability to arrive at knowledge that will resolve disputes. There is a note of hope in the ability to overcome disagreements. Yet, there is a fear that if a majority does in fact come to have knowledge about basic matters, then there is the danger of persecution of the minority. Such a system is not suited to the growth in knowledge about basic matters but is grounded in philosophical skepticism.

3 COMMON SENSE AND THE SELF-EVIDENT IN LAW

In the 1965 Supreme Court case *United States v. Seeger*, a conscientious objector who was not a member of a recognized religious denomination tested the Court's understanding and definition of "religion." In this case, we see the application of recognizing ongoing factions within the country. About religious belief, the Court said, "The test of religious belief within the meaning of the exemption in sec. 6(j) is whether it is a sincere and meaningful belief occupying in the life of its possessor a place parallel to that filled by the god of those admittedly qualified for the exemption."[1] In order to decide the case, the Court reasoned,

> The parties raise the basic question of the constitutionality of the section which defines the term "religious training and belief," as used in the act, as "an individual's belief in a relation to a supreme being involving duties superior to those arising from any human relation but not including essentially political, sociological, or philosophical views or a merely personal moral code." The constitutional attack is launched under the first amendment's establishment and free exercise clauses and is twofold: (1) the section does not exempt nonreligious conscientious objectors; and (2) it discriminates between different forms of religious expression in violation of the due process clause of the fifth amendment... because his opposition to war is based on belief in a supreme reality and is therefore an obligation superior to one resulting from man's relationship to his fellow man. Peter contends that his opposition to war derives from his acceptance of the existence of a universal power beyond that of man and that this acceptance in fact constitutes belief in a supreme being, qualifying him for exemption.[2]

The outcome was a more precise definition of religion. Rather than defining "religion" in a theistic way that excludes nontheistic religions, the Court gave a definition that sees the role of religious beliefs as giving answers to the basic questions that humans ask. It said,

> We have concluded that congress, in using the expression "supreme being" rather than the designation "god," was merely clarifying the meaning of religious training and belief so as to embrace all religions and to exclude essentially political, sociological, or philosophical views. We believe that under this construction, the test of belief "in a relation to a supreme being" is whether a given belief that is sincere and meaningful occupies a place in the life of its possessor parallel to that filled by the orthodox belief in god of one who clearly qualifies for the exemption.[3]

And yet behind this reasoning, there remains the skepticism that we have seen earlier. Rather than nesting it in the limits of the government, the Court continued to discuss the issue in a way that shows it recognizes the differences in religious claims, that these differences involve giving competing answers to basic questions, and that this is an area in which knowledge is most elusive:

> Few would quarrel, we think, with the proposition that in no field of human endeavor has the tool of language proved so inadequate in the communication of ideas as it has in dealing with the fundamental questions of man's predicament in life, in death or in final judgment and retribution. This fact makes the task of discerning the intent of congress in using the phrase "supreme being" a complex one. Nor is it made the easier by the richness and variety of spiritual life in our country. Over 250 sects inhabit our land. Some believe in a purely personal god, some in a supernatural deity; others think of religion as a way of life envisioning as its ultimate goal the day when all men can live together in perfect understanding and peace. There are those who think of god as the depth of our being; others, such as the Buddhists, strive for a state of lasting rest through self-denial and inner purification; in Hindu philosophy, the supreme being is the transcendental reality which is truth, knowledge and bliss. Even those religious groups which have traditionally opposed war in every form have splintered into various denominations.[4]

The recognition of these sects, or factions, is one level of analysis. Clearly, there are such factions and divisions. However, the decision goes beyond recognizing this and stating the limits of government in dealing with people coming to agreement about basic questions. Instead, the Court said,

> And in so doing it is also significant that Congress did not elaborate on the form or nature of this higher authority which it chose to designate as 'supreme being.' By so refraining it must have had in mind the admonitions of the chief justice when he said in the same opinion that even the word 'god' had myriad meanings for men of faith.[5]

In saying this, it even cites Paul Tillich, who will we consider in more depth in another chapter: "Moreover, we believe this construction embraces the ever broadening understanding of the modern religious community. The eminent protestant theologian, Dr. Paul Tillich, whose views the government concedes would come within the statute, identifies god not as a projection 'out there' or beyond the skies but as the ground of our very being."[6]

Recognizing that the state cannot use force to encourage unity nor can it step over its limits into the realm of the truth of religious belief, it nevertheless rests on an epistemology of religious experience that is grounded in skepticism about our ability to know the truth about what is real and the highest good:

> The validity of what he believes cannot be questioned. Some theologians, and indeed some examiners, might be tempted to question the existence of the registrant's "supreme being" or the truth of his concepts. But these are inquiries foreclosed to government. As Mr. Justice Douglas stated … "men may believe what they cannot prove. They may not be put to the proof of their religious doctrines or beliefs. Religious experiences which are as real as life to some may be incomprehensible to others." Local boards and courts in this sense are not free to reject beliefs because they consider them "incomprehensible." Their task is to decide whether the beliefs professed by a registrant are sincerely held and whether they are, in his own scheme of things, religious.[7]

In the earlier chapters, we saw the dichotomy between tradition and religious experience that has recurred in American history. Taking religious experience as a source of knowledge or as a source of recalcitrant opinion that leads to divisions that cannot be overcome is an influential epistemology in American thinking about religion and law. In order to analyze it, we will look at the influence of Thomas Reid. He gave an account of knowledge, including knowledge of God and the good, that was influential in the early republic and has seen a resurgence of influence in the past three decades.

THOMAS REID

We have already seen Thomas Reid relied on by contemporary philosophers to give a response to skepticism. Reid is the founder of the school of Scottish Common Sense Philosophy. This philosophy was influential on the thinking of the Founders through schools like Princeton and professors like John Witherspoon. Many teachers came from Scotland and brought this philosophy with them. It was a powerful response to the skepticism of David Hume. It continued to be the philosophy of America deep into the nineteenth century. However, it continued to rely on categories developed by the British Empiricists:

> For Locke perception involves three elements: the percipient, the idea perceived, and the thing; and it is assumed that the idea is somehow a copy of the external reality. Both Berkeley and Reid saw clearly the difficulties of the doctrine of Representative Perception. If the mind is confined to its own ideas and is cut off from immediate knowledge of the real world, how is it to know if its ideas do or do not agree with things? In order to compare two things, it is necessary to know both. Thus we cannot compare ideas with the things which they represent, because we can never escape the circle of our own ideas. And the further objection is advanced that if the external world does exist, it cannot be like our ideas, for nothing but an idea can be like an idea. Both Berkeley and Reid saw these difficulties in Locke's doctrine. They both agreed that Locke had gone wrong. How he had gone wrong was the question on which they differed ... By Berkeley it was maintained that Locke's third factor – the material world – had no real existence. But Reid denied the existence of Locke's second factor. Locke's imitative and intermediate ideas are simply creatures of phantasy: they have no real existence. Thus Berkeley is left with mind plus ideas, and

> Reid with mind plus matter. For both, the relation between mind and its object is immediate.[8]

Thomas Reid argued that there are self-evident first principles that are presupposed in all knowledge and thinking. He identifies first principles in metaphysics and ethics. First, we are going to look at what he says and then consider how it compares to the claims in the Declaration of Independence and if it has indeed given us self-evident first principles.

Reid's philosophy is motivated by the skepticism of David Hume. Hume was the last of the British Empiricists. Beginning with John Locke, these philosophers believed that all knowledge is from experience. The contribution of Hume was to show how this leads to the inability to know anything. Hume used the standards of empiricism to show that we cannot know causation, the self, or whether the future will be like the past. He reduced morality to the desire for pleasure rather than the pursuit of the good. Reid is notable in not only seeing the threat that Hume posed to all philosophy and religion but in developing a response that many continue to use today. About Hume, Reid said,

> Philosophy is indebted to Mr. Hume in this respect among others, that, by calling in question many of the first principles of human knowledge, he hath put speculative men upon inquiring more carefully than was done before, into the nature of the evidence upon which they rest. Truth can never suffer by a fair inquiry; it can bear to be seen naked and in the fullest light; and the strictest examination will always turn out in the issue to its advantage. I believe Mr. Hume was the first who ever called in question whether things that begin to exist must have a cause.[9]

Reid gives an example of how he justifies first principles by noting that if they are denied, then all philosophy, religion, and reasoning ends. If the belief that whatever begins to exist has a cause is a mere opinion, then there is no ability to continue reasoning about anything. He says, "The first of these suppositions would put an end to all philosophy, to all religion, to all reasoning that would carry us beyond the objects of sense, and to all prudence in the conduct of life."[10]

It is this standard that Reid uses to explain his first principles. He calls them "common sense," but he does not mean that they are the collected opinions of the uneducated. Instead, they are what is necessary for discussion and thought to continue. He phrases it this way:

> All men that have common understanding agree in such principles, and consider a man as lunatic, or destitute of common sense, who denies or calls them in question. Thus, if any man were found of so strange a turn as not to believe his own eyes; to put no trust in his senses, nor have the least regard to their testimony; would any man think it worth while to reason gravely with such a person, and, by argument, to convince him of his error? Surely no wise man would. For before men can reason together, they must agree in first principles; and it is impossible to reason with a man who has no principles in common with you. There are, therefore, common principles, which are the foundation of all reasoning, and of all science.[11]

The idea that knowledge begins with first principles has been strongly critiqued in the time since Thomas Reid. One critique is that from the psychological perspective of how a person reports forming beliefs, this simply does not seem to be true. However, we need to keep the distinction between psychology and epistemology clear. It is true that the British Empiricists beginning with Locke were often doing psychology in that they believed themselves to be describing how people start with sense data and arrive at beliefs from there. Some of Reid's philosophy can be taken this way. However, epistemology as the study of knowledge is interested not primarily in how people form beliefs, since many or even most of these beliefs are false. Instead, epistemology is interested in how we can have knowledge in contrast with opinion or false belief.

The other criticism is that there are not such first principles. We considered this criticism earlier from Alvin Plantinga. However, rather than thinking in terms of first principles, we can think of laws of thought. These are the laws that make thought possible. Whether one believes there are first principles or not does not affect the reality of laws of thought. We can distinguish thought from nonthought, and in doing so, we can identify the laws that make this distinction. A violation of these laws leads to the meaninglessness of a purported thought. The supposed thought in question might have the appearance of meaning, but upon examination, if it violates a law of thought, then it is not actually meaningful.

There is a sense in which Reid is looking for something like the laws of thought. He understands many of his first principles as the necessary conditions for thought itself. It is this sense in which they are common to all people, or *common sense*. In Reid the phrase common sense and the idea of first principles can have different meanings or senses:

> With regard to Reid one could get the impression that there are at least five different senses of common sense in Reid, namely using words as agreeably as possible to their common use in language, what is common in the respective phenomenon's nature, epistemic common sense realism, perceptual common sense realism, and common judgment. Yet Reid makes it abundantly clear that sense in its most proper meaning means judgment, so that common sense actually means common judgment.... Reid usually meant certain propositions believed in common with his phrase "principles of common sense," but sometimes also meant certain belief-forming faculties shared in common. Reid distinguishes between first principles of contingent truths, first principles of necessary truths, and first principles in morals.[12]

This last sense that there are belief-forming faculties that all humans share in common is itself part of a larger anthropology, or belief about human nature and origins. Humans were made with senses, or faculties, that give accurate information and, therefore, form true or warranted beliefs. This means that such a view assumes that humans were indeed created in this way.

> The common theological heritage of the moral cognitivists of the eighteenth century helps to explain why these commitments were so widely held. The "Westminster Confession of Faith," to which at least the Scottish professors were expected to subscribe, maintains that: After God had made all other creatures, He created man, male and female, with reasonable and immortal souls, endued with knowledge, righteousness, and true holiness, after His own image; having the law of God written in their hearts, and power to fulfill it ....[13]

Included in this anthropology is the reality that humans are currently in a fallen and sinful condition. "While this description applies to humanity before the Fall, both Presbyterian and Anglican doctrine maintained that the imago was only corrupted and not altogether lost in the fall of the race. Part of the retained image was the power of moral discernment."[14] Since the Fall did not completely corrupt the human belief-forming faculties, in some sense, they are still reliable, although in other respects, they no longer give the right beliefs. This is especially true when it comes to beliefs about God and the good. A criticism of this is that it makes the reality of unbelief an issue of faulty belief-forming faculties for which one is not responsible. It is in part due to this criticism that the belief of free will as the ability to do otherwise became influential, although this is not the only way to respond to this objection.

To call a moral theory "cognitivist" is to say that moral beliefs can be analyzed as either true or false. The prevalent moral theory in Reid's day was the following:

> The "hard core" of the eighteenth-century cognitivist programme in moral philosophy can be summarized in five assumptions: (A1) We are capable of acting from other-regarding motives. (A2) The world possesses irreducibly moral features that are not imposed by, even though they are bound up in, our volitions. (A3) Even though the moral features of the world are neither arbitrary nor liable to capricious revision, God, the author of creation, is solely responsible for their existence. (A4) Even though moral duty and virtue are conceptually distinct from omniscient self-interest, God freely chose to order the world in such a way that the two are coextensive. (A5) God has endowed us with the capacity to discern the moral features of the world necessary for living upright lives. All five of these assumptions were considered to be beyond negotiation by the eighteenth-century Scottish and English authors upon whom Reid relied in his work on morals and the moral life.[15]

We can see these assumptions in Reid's own thought. His influence on early Americans has been well documented. So, too, has his role in responding to David Hume's radical empiricism and consequent skepticism. Reid's response to skepticism involved showing that there are some truths which can be known and do not need proof. "As there are words common to Philosophers and to the vulgar, which need no explication, so there are principles common to both which need no proof, and which do not admit of direct proof."[16] That there are such truths is a truth that he did not think required further proof: "I take it for granted, that there are self-evident principles. Nobody, I think, denies it. And if any man were so sceptical as to deny that there is any proposition that is self-evident, I see not how it would be possible to convince him by reasoning."[17]

Reid recognizes that there is a difference of opinion about first principles and what is thought to be self-evident. "But yet there seems to be great difference of opinions among philosophers about first principles. What one takes to be self-evident, another labours to prove by arguments, and a third denies altogether."[18] He gives an approach on how to arrive at agreement about first principles and settle disputes in order to have unity. These involve showing that it is absurd to deny certain self-evident truths. This absurdity ends up in denying what must be assumed and in recognizing that a person is pressed by the very fact of being a human to accept what is indeed self-evident. "Thus I conceive, that first principles, which are really the dictates of common sense, and directly opposed to absurdities in opinion, will always, from the constitution of human nature, support themselves, and gain rather than lose ground among mankind."[19]

Next, and related, is that it becomes self-refuting to reject some first principles:

> A first principle may admit of a proof ad absurdum. In this kind of proof, which is very common in mathematics, we suppose the contradictory proposition to be true. We trace the consequences of that supposition in a train of reasoning; and if we find any of its necessary consequences to be manifestly absurd, we conclude the supposition from which it followed to be false; and therefore its contradictory to be true.[20]

It is in this sense that Reid sees himself as identifying the very principles that are necessary for thought itself.

The first place to start is that there are indeed first principles that are certain. "First, I hold it to be certain, and even demonstrable, That all knowledge got by reasoning must be built upon first principles. This is as certain as that every house must have a foundation."[21] In using terms like "foundation," students of philosophy will think of "foundationalism" as a particular branch of epistemology. However, it would be a mistake to identify Reid in that way at this point. If he is working to identify the necessary truths for thought itself, then these are relevant whether one is a foundationalist or a coherentist. The reason for identifying these principles is to better understand knowledge itself and the various ways it is grounded in what is self-evident.[22] In doing this, we can reach the goal of attaining unity among persons and overcoming the various divisions that remain between humans.

> Nature hath not left us destitute of means whereby the candid and honest part of mankind may be brought to unanimity when they happen to differ about first principles. When men differ about things that are taken to be first principles or self-evident truths, reasoning seems to be at an end. Each party appeals to common sense. When one man's common sense gives one determination, another man's a contrary determination, there seems to be no remedy but to leave every man to enjoy his own opinion. This is a common observation, and I believe a just one, if it be rightly understood. It is in vain to reason with a man who denies the first principles on which the reasoning is grounded. Thus, it would be in vain to attempt the proof of a proposition in Euclid to a man who denies the axioms. Indeed, we ought never to reason with men who deny first principles from obstinacy and unwillingness to yield to reason. But is it not possible, that men who really love truth, and are open to conviction, may differ about first principles? I think it is possible, and that it cannot, without great want of charity, be denied to be possible.[23]

First principles form a common ground for thinking together. If there is no common ground, then there can be no way to move forward in agreement. In order to uncover where a disagreement lies, he gives what we might call a presuppositional approach: "In all rational belief, the thing believed is (1) either itself a first principle, or (2) it is by just reasoning deduced from first-principles. When men differ, about deductions of reasoning, the appeal must be made to the rules of reasoning."[24] By tracing back the origin of the disagreement to first principles, we can see exactly where the disagreement began and what it is about at the most basic level. In most cases, attention is given to disagreements and the divisions they cause at a less basic level. Reid proposes that this can be avoided by thinking in terms of the relationship of these disagreements to their first principles.

Reid believed there were first principles in morality, and we can consider these for their own sake but also apply them in a way to the ethics of belief. He says, "Men may be highly culpable in omitting what they ought to have done, as well as in doing what they ought not."[25] If we think of this in terms of belief, it means that there are beliefs we ought to hold and also beliefs that we are culpable for not holding. We should know some things. Taken with his claims about the role of first principles in resolving disputes, we ought to know what is most basic. We can know these if we have taken the time to think about them: "These principles concerning virtue and vice in general, must appear self-evident to every man who hath a conscience, and who hath taken pains to exercise this natural power of his mind. I proceed to others that are more particular."[26] Therefore, if we do not know them, it is only because we have not been seeking to know. Consequently, there is no one to blame for our ignorance about basic things but ourselves.

In terms of morality, it is self-evident that "we ought to prefer a greater good, though more distant, to a less; and a less evil to a greater."[27] The fact that there is a difference between greater and lesser goods means that there is a greatest good. If there is only an infinite expanse of goods, then one cannot be said to be greater or lesser since one cannot get closer to infinity. Reid himself speaks of virtue as a kind of public good and happiness as a kind of private good. "If a man can be induced to do his duty even from a regard to his own happiness, he will soon find reason to love virtue for her own sake, and to act from motives less mercenary. I cannot therefore approve of those moralists who would banish all persuasives to virtue taken from the consideration of private good."[28] As is common, he ultimately thinks of the highest good as a kind of happiness achieved in the afterlife. This belief contributes to dividing religious belief from achieving the good in this life.

Reid's account of how beliefs are formed relies on his beliefs about God. "The Author of our being hath given us not only the power of acting within a limited sphere, but various principles or springs of action, of different nature and dignity, to direct us in the exercise of our active power."[29] It is important to note that he does not make belief in God a first principle. He does make belief in causation and belief in the relationship between the sign of intelligence and the reality of intelligence first principles. These can be developed into the cosmological and teleological arguments. Contemporary followers of Reid, like Plantinga, infuse God into their definition of warranted belief by saying it is based on a design plan aimed at truth. The assumption is that there is a designer with a design plan. In his system, Reid leaves God as an assumption to support his epistemology. Even if he can develop a cosmological or teleological argument, the principles on which such an argument would rest assume that there is an "Author" of our being, as the above quote shows. Therefore, they are circular.

In an interesting quote, Reid does say that there are some self-evident truths related to God once a person believes in God's existence:

> To every man who believes the existence, the perfections, and the providence of God, the veneration and submission we owe to him is self-evident. Right sentiments of the Deity and of his works, not only make the duty we owe to him obvious to every intelligent being, but likewise add the authority of a divine law to every rule of right conduct.[30]

This does not help settle disputes about how God is to be worshiped, an area that divides Christians in Reid's day and throughout American history. Nor does it tell us what the "right sentiments" are that should be had toward God.

It is possible to mistake something as a first principle that is not. "It is so irksome to reason with those who deny first principles, that wise men commonly decline it. Yet it is not impossible, that what is only a vulgar prejudice may be mistaken for a first principle."[31] The consequence of not correctly identifying first principles or attempting to prove what are actually first principles by other supposedly more evident principles is skepticism.

> Though it has not been usual, yet I conceive it may be useful, to point out some of those things which I shall take for granted, as first principles, in treating of the mind and its faculties. There is the more occasion for this; because very ingenious men, such as Des Cartes, Malebranche, Arnauld, Locke, and many others, have lost much labour by not distinguishing things which require proof, from things which, though they may admit of illustration, yet being

> self-evident, do not admit of proof. When men attempt to deduce such self-evident principles from others more evident, they always fall into inconclusive reasoning: And the consequence of this has been, that others, such as Berkeley and Hume, finding the arguments brought to prove such first principles to be weak and inconclusive, have been tempted first to doubt of them, and afterwards to deny them.[32]

The implication is: "There are, therefore, common principles, which are the foundation of all reasoning, and of all science. Such common principles seldom admit of direct proof, nor do they need it. Men need not to be taught them; for they are such as all men of common understanding know; or such, at least, as they give a ready assent to, as soon as they are proposed and understood."[33]

> Thus, if any man were found of so strange a turn as not to believe his own eyes; to put no trust in his senses, nor have the least regard to their testimony; would any man think it worth while to reason gravely with such a person, and, by argument, to convince him of his error? Surely no wise man would. For before men can reason together, they must agree in first principles; and it is impossible to reason with a man who has no principles in common with you.[34]

This idea that it is impossible to reason with a man who has no principles in common with you helps shed light on the motivation of the Declaration of Independence. It makes its argument for the world to understand the revolution. It begins its argument with what is taken to be self-evident. These are the first principles of the revolution and include that it is self-evident that there is a Creator. They serve as axioms. Reid describes these in the following way:

> But there are other propositions which are no sooner understood than they are believed. The judgment follows the apprehension of them necessarily, and both are equally the work of nature, and the result of our original powers. There is no searching for evidence, no weighing of arguments; the proposition is not deduced or inferred from another; it has the light of truth in itself, and has no occasion to borrow it from another. Propositions of the last kind, when they are used in matters of science, have commonly been called axioms.[35]

Some of these logical axioms are that not every compilation of words has meaning, that a proposition is either true or false, that no proposition can be both true and false at the same time, that circular reasoning proves nothing, and that anything that can be affirmed of a genus can be affirmed of the individual species of that genus.[36]

Because we are looking at the claim that it is self-evident that God exists, we can turn to Reid's claims about the first principles of metaphysics.

> The last class of first principles I shall mention, we may call metaphysical. I shall particularly consider three of these, because they have been called in question by Mr. Hume. The first is, That the qualities which we perceive by our senses must have a subject, which we call body, and that the thoughts we are conscious of must have a subject, which we call mind.[37]

Next is that whatever begins to exist must have a cause.[38] The next is that from design in the effect we may infer design or intelligence in the cause.[39]

These can be understood to be common sense in that everyone believes them, however unconsciously. Or in that everyone would give assent to them when they are brought to mind. Or that they are the necessary prerequisites for knowing anything else. This last forms a kind of transcendental argument that searches for the necessary preconditions of a subject, in this case knowledge.

This idea of common sense providing the starting place for knowledge became influential in American thought, although not always in the same sophisticated manner outlined by Reid. Appeals to common sense can run the gamut from mere assertions of opinion to the generally accepted opinions of a group of people at a specific time to claims about what all people must believe universally. It is the latter that is important for natural theology. Claims about what all people believe are not empirical due to the reality that this would require that all people be interviewed. Many people are dead, others are yet to be born, and those living are scattered over the Earth. Therefore, it must be a claim about the nature of thought itself.

As a claim about thought, it is looking to identify and articulate the laws of thought. These laws define thought and are authoritative over what is a meaningful and not a meaningful thought. However, the term *reason* can be used to mean "common sense" itself or intuition or reasoning. These all are less basic than reason as the laws of thought and presuppose that we can indeed identify reason as the laws of thought so as then to go on and identify how it relates to common sense, intuition, and the reasoning process.

The influence of what came to be called Scottish Realism was undeniable after the Revolution and up until the Civil War.

> The Scottish method was brought to America by President John Witherspoon of Princeton, and came into absolute domination of academic curricula by about 1820 .... The Presbyterian Church made the Scottish doctrine virtually synonymous with Protestantism, with the result that the other denominations, even the most Evangelical, incorporated it into their teaching when their institutions also offered courses in "philosophy." During all these years, it was resolutely unaffected by the idealistic movements which ran riot in Europe, and it especially set a stern face of disapproval against the flutter of literary Idealism among the Transcendental fraternity of New England.[40]

It is also remarkable that this influence waned so quickly after the Civil War so that its influence could hardly be found by the twentieth century.

> It is a curious fact that one of the most radical revolutions in the history of American mind took place in the two or three decades after the Civil War without exciting appreciable comment: the philosophy and the philosophers of Scottish Realism vanished from the American colleges, leaving not even a rack behind, and were swiftly replaced by expounders of some form of Idealism.[41]

Perry Miller explains the motivation for accepting this realism:

> This Realism could be so widely and uncritically accepted because, for one reason, it was based upon John Locke; during the Revolution, America had embraced him as its own political theorist and moralist. For another and more important reason, Scottish Realism was a philosophy of "common sense" – forthright, down-to-earth, rational, and yet pious. It supported orthodoxy in theology, raised no dangerous questions, invited no intellectual adventures. It was enlightened, and yet conservative. It was a restatement of Locke against David Hume, and contradicted Hume's skepticism by a blanket assertion that idea and object correspond so faithfully that

> Americans, intent upon their business, need never give a second thought to so unprofitable worry.[42]

It is interesting that he sees it not as a new response to Hume but as a restatement of John Locke's empiricism in an attempt to answer Hume's skepticism. Empiricism was retained, but the emphasis on ideas as mediators between the world and the mind was dropped. Instead, humans have direct access to the world through sense data. This epistemology could then be used to formulate arguments for God's existence based on causation or design.

The American thinkers were often contrasted with the Europeans as being less sophisticated in their understanding of philosophy. They relied on commonsense realism to defend Christian belief long after it had been abandoned on the Continent for Kantianism and Hegelianism. Both Kant and Hegel claimed to be providing a defense of Christianity in their systems, but it was not the orthodox Christianity of the Reformation summarized in the Westminster Confession of Faith. It relied on Christian terminology but was instead either a defense of deontology (Kant) or a kind of idealism/pantheism (Hegel). American thought could not be kept from this influence, and the question is why it became popular in the last part of the nineteenth century.

> Nevertheless, this American ideology crumbled rapidly after 1870 and by 1890 had disappeared – except as it might survive in the dogmatic assurances of politicians and preachers. One may say that it expired mainly because the behemoths of the system failed to train up successors, so that with the death of McCosh in 1894 there was no one to carry on. But a more cogent reason is the fact that younger intellects – even those who might otherwise have been temperamentally sympathetic with Bowen, Porter, and McCosh – realized that in the rapidly altering circumstances a naïve Realism was no longer a match for the two challenges which so pressed upon the culture that America could no longer live in philosophical isolation. These were, first, the thrust of organized Idealism, particularly in its Hegelian and post-Hegelian formulations, and second, the devastating upset of the Scottish methods of reasoning contained in Charles Darwin's *The Origin of Species*, published in 1859.[43]

The connection of Darwinism to Hegelian process theology is important because it helps us understand that Darwinism, claiming to be empirical, was a rationalist system that imposed an interpretation on the empirical data in keeping with the presuppositions of naturalism (all events must be explained by material causes) and process thought (change occurs through gradual alterations from the distant past into the distant future). "God" was still a point of reference, but this was no longer the God of theism. It was sometimes the God of deism, who creates a system and then is no longer involved. More often it was the God of pantheism, who is identified with the system itself.

CONCLUSION

The outcome is a conflict between worldviews that continues to the present. No longer could it be claimed that it is self-evident that humans are created. Common sense as a defense of the existence of God and the doctrines of Christianity had lost its authority. No doubt common sense and religious experience continued to be appealed to by Christians in support of their beliefs. But they were also sources of authority used by those rejecting Christianity. Common sense and experience were not sufficient to resolve disputes that ultimately traced to competing answers to basic questions. Instead, these must be tested by reason for coherence. Naturalism, as the belief that only the material world exists and that only material causes can be used in explanations, faces important philosophical challenges. It is an old philosophy dating to the Greek materialists. Yet in its new form, it took an air of authority under the name of science that dismissed theological and religious inquiry as outdated.

Thus, a new faction was added to the list of those competing for influence in American thought. The Madisonian solution of pitting faction against faction remained the pragmatic answer. Each worldview can appeal to what it takes to be common sense and to its interpretation of experience but with no effect in convincing the other or of resolving the dispute. When the government and law are called upon to arbitrate these divisions, the solution will remain pragmatic.

4 INTUITION AND THE SELF-EVIDENT IN LAW

During World War I, there was a backlash against all things German. This included the German language and Lutheran churches, where the worry was that German propaganda was being taught under the guise of religion. In the case *Meyer v. Nebraska*, the Supreme Court decided a case in which the German language was being taught to schoolchildren at a private school using Bible stories. The Fourteenth Amendment was cited to defend this practice in that "No state ... shall deprive any person of life, liberty or property without due process of law." Justice Reynolds maintained,

> Without doubt, it denotes not merely freedom from bodily restraint but also the right of the individual to contract, to engage in any of the common occupations of life, to acquire useful knowledge, to marry, establish a home and bring up children, to worship God according to the dictates of his own conscience, and generally to enjoy those privileges long recognizes at common law as essential to the orderly pursuit of happiness by free men.[1]

This liberty is not to be interfered with by the state in the name of protecting the public interest without demonstration of some reasonable relation to a state purpose within the sphere of the state's influence.

We have already seen divisions between Unitarians and Trinitarians. More cases emerged as more divisions arose within Christianity, and with new religious movements such as Mormonism and Jehovah's Witnesses. One of the issues surrounding Jehovah's Witnesses was their distribution of religious material door to door. In *Cantwell v. Connecticut* (1940), the conflict was between the state's obligation to protect order and peace within its borders and the freedom to distribute religious opinions. The justice decided that the defendant's distribution of literature did not amount to a breach of the peace. However, the justice did maintain that

> In the realm of religious faith, and in that of political belief, sharp differences arise. In both fields the tenets of one man may seem the rankest error to his neighbor ... But the people of this nation have ordained in the light of history, that, in spite of the probability of excesses and abuses, these liberties are, in the long view, essential to enlightened opinion and right conduct on the part of the citizens of a democracy ... Nowhere is this shield more necessary than in our own country for a people composed of many races and of many creeds.[2]

These decisions recognize the reality of the important role religious beliefs play for the individual, of their divisive nature when there are disagreements, and of the increased division through diversity of religious beliefs. If religious beliefs are necessary for the well-being of civil society, does it matter which religious beliefs these are? If the state depends on religious teaching for the virtue of its citizens, does it also depend on which religious beliefs and virtues are being taught? What seems to come out in these decisions is that the state is unable to make any determinations in this area while also being dependent on religion. This may indeed be a limitation of the powers of the state. However, it may also be true that the state depends on religious teaching. The implication is that as divisions continue, the state is both unable to resolve these and the well-being of society is put in jeopardy. Maintaining liberty of individual belief is important but does not comment on the role true religious belief plays in supporting the state. The outcome is increasingly that the state must not depend on religions since these are so badly divided.

The divisions followed a line of challenges. They began with challenges about the nature of God (Trinitarian and Unitarian). New religious movements emerged that also challenged the nature of God, claiming either that God was once a man (Mormonism) or affirming that Christ was the first created being but not equal to God (Jehovah's Witnesses). In this sense, the challenges are all about special revelation and about the nature of God and what can be known of God. Furthermore, they are challenges about what must be known of God to lead the good life. As such, they propose very different visions of the good life and of what constitutes virtue. If the state relies on religion to teach virtue and yet the existing religions in the state are badly divided on these issues, then the state must look elsewhere for what it considers to be a virtuous citizenry. This idea increasingly became a very broad sense of the pursuit of happiness while not interfering with the pursuit of happiness of others. It no longer included the idea of teaching about a future life since this was dependent on doctrines that were in dispute.

RALPH WALDO EMERSON

We are going to look at the work of Emerson in order to understand how ideas about *God* changed and multiplied during the nineteenth century. Emerson was Harvard educated and began his career as a Unitarian minister. However, he soon found even that denomination too restrictive and became a proponent, even a chief thinker, of the movement called Transcendentalism.

Because of his rhetorical style, he often speaks of God and even Christianity in a way that sounds familiar to orthodox Protestants. However, as we look at his ideas, we will see that he taught a kind of pantheism, that all is God, that each person contains the divine, and the we can come into contact with this divinity through a kind of intuition and religious experience. In a speech to Harvard students, he said,

> What is nature to him? There is never a beginning, there is never an end, to the inexplicable continuity of this web of God, but always circular power returning into itself. Therein it resembles his own spirit, whose beginning, whose ending, he never can find, – so entire, so boundless.[3]

This speech was well received, and it makes us wonder if the audience understood what Emerson was saying. There is never a beginning or an end to what Emerson calls "nature;" it is eternal like God because it is God. Furthermore, the human spirit is also without beginning and without end. It, too, is equated with God. It, too, is eternal. Christianity maintains that the human spirit has no end but that it was created by God and, therefore, had a beginning. But here Emerson affirms that all is eternal; nature, the soul, and God are eternal. All is one. In this way, Emerson is rejecting the claim that it is self-evident that God created. Rather, nothing is created but is instead part of a system or cycle of divinity.

Emerson identifies Transcendentalism with Idealism. This is the belief that the mind and its ideas are real and that the material world is but an appearance. He says,

> What is popularly called Transcendentalism among us, is Idealism; Idealism as it appears in 1842. As thinkers, mankind have ever divided into two sects, Materialists and Idealists; the first class founding on experience, the second on consciousness; the first class beginning to think from the data of the senses, the second class perceive that the senses are not final, and say, the senses give us representations of things, but what are the things themselves.[4]

Idealism is not new with Emerson. The problem of how to know the difference between appearance and reality was a problem dating to the earliest philosophers. There has tended to be a swing in the history of philosophy between those who claim that the material world is ultimate reality and those who claim that mind is the ultimate reality. This debate involves questions both about how we know and about what is real. Because we are directly aware of our mind but only indirectly aware of the material world, the idealist says that the mental world is more real.

Because God created the material world and is a spirit, this form of idealism takes the step to say that all spirit is divine or a part of God. The distinction between God as an eternal spirit and the human as a created spirit is lost. Ultimately, all is one. Emerson notes that this form of idealism has been influential in Eastern philosophy:

> The oriental mind has always tended to this largeness. Buddhism is an expression of it. The Buddhist, who thanks no man, who says "Do not flatter your benefactors," but who, in his conviction that every good deed can by no possibility escape its reward, will not deceive the benefactor by pretending that he has done more than he should, is a Transcendentalist.[5]

Many of the writings of Eastern religions were becoming translated and more readily accessible at the time of Emerson. Emerson himself was greatly influenced by the Bhagavad Gita. This is a Hindu text in which Krishna teaches that the world and the self are not real. Through the process of reincarnation, each person can seek unity with ultimate reality, which is pure consciousness.

Clearly this is not the same as theism. That does not make it false, but it does stand in contrast to the idea that all humans are created. Since Emerson uses the term *God*, many were not able, or perhaps not willing, to note the difference in meaning he gave to this word. Others were undoubtedly eager to see the meaning of the word change.

It is worthwhile to note that Emerson appeals to the same religious experience that earlier Christians like Jonathan Edwards had used in the First Great Awakening:

> The rationalistic mind seemed to him to have chilled and rigidified the whole of human existence, beginning with the life of the spirit on its profoundest levels. His own religious experience, like that of his grandfather in the days of Edwards and Whitefield, had taught him that religion has far less to do with the "understanding" than with what Edwards called "an affected fervent heart," and that without "a certain enthusiasm," as Emerson himself said, it is nothing. The cool, reasonable, philosophical beliefs of the Deists and of many Unitarians seemed to him a spiritless substitute for religion, not religion itself: thus for him was "an influx of the Divine mind into our mind" an ecstasy, not an induction. With institutions, with churches, with creeds and liturgies, it has at best only secondary relations. Essentially it is a superrational communication between the individual soul and what Emerson came to call the Over-Soul.[6]

In keeping with the influence of Eastern philosophy, Emerson embraces contradiction. It was Emerson who said that "consistency is the hobgoblin of little minds." Reality is fundamentally contradictory, and therefore reason cannot comprehend it. Instead, we must go beyond reason to intuition. Because reason, as the laws of thought, is the foundation for any meaningful belief or statement, there is finally no way to express reality in a meaningful way. Reason, as the laws of thought such as noncontradiction, and cognitive meaning must be set aside in favor of intuition and the flow of noncognitive experience.

> He will never be understood by readers who fail to take in that the is a consciously "dialectical" thinker – one, that is, who holds that contradiction is inherent in experience itself, that the natural order is through and through paradoxical, and that we shall never comprehend it truly until we have learned to "keep the diagonal line."[7]

In contrast to reason, Emerson relies on the faculty of intuition. This can be an ambiguous term. It usually means an immediate awareness in which we connect a sign with reality or take a sign to be reality. One might believe that something bad is going to happen because of a nervous feeling; one might believe a person is friendly because of a smile; one might believe that God exists because of a beautiful sunset; or one might believe that God does not exist because of a scene of devastation. The act of intuition is in the immediate connection between these rather than a process of inference. Intuition is often related to feelings, or sentiments, in that feelings are taken to accurately reflect reality. Emerson says,

> The intuition of the moral sentiment is an insight of the perfection of the laws of the soul. These laws execute themselves. They are out of time, out of space, and not subject to circumstance. Thus in the soul of man there is a justice whose retributions are instant and entire. He who does a good deed is instantly ennobled. He who does a mean deed is by the action itself contracted. He who puts off impurity, thereby puts on purity. If a man is at heart just, then in so far is he God; the safety of God, the immortality of God, the majesty of God do enter into that man with justice.[8]

Emerson argues that this intuition or perception of the law also gives us a religious feeling that connects us to our highest happiness and is itself divine: "The perception of this law of laws awakens in the mind a sentiment which we call the religious sentiment, and which makes our highest happiness...This sentiment is divine and deifying. It is the beatitude of man ... This sentiment lies at the foundation of society, and successively creates all forms of worship."[9]

It is on this basis that Emerson criticizes historic Christianity. If personal intuitions are the individual's connection to the highest reality, then this individual experience cannot be communicated to others. It is entirely particular and individual. It is, according to Emerson, the realization of the divinity of the self.

> In this point of view we become sensible of the first defect of historical Christianity. Historical Christianity has fallen into the error that corrupts all attempts to communicate religion. As it appears to us, and as it has appeared for ages, it is not the doctrine of the soul, but an exaggeration of the personal, the positive, the ritual ... That is always best which gives me to myself. The sublime so excited in me by the great stoical doctrine, Obey thyself. That which shows God in me, fortifies me.[10]

Emerson links historic Christianity with "tradition" and calls the latter "dead." He even anticipates Nietzsche in speaking about "God is dead." Here we should distinguish between tradition and historic Christianity. Tradition can mean the values handed down over time. It can also mean the continued use of rituals and stories that are emptied of meaning. By way of contrast, historic Christianity means the teaching of the pastors/teachers of the Christian faith summarized in the creeds as they address current challenges after much discussion. This means that historic Christianity is anything but "dead;" it is active in addressing challenges. What counts as historic Christianity are the teachings, summarized in creeds, consistent with the teaching of the apostles dating to the first council in Jerusalem. This council, recounted in Acts 15, addressed the challenges of what it means to be a Christian: if the sign of circumcision is necessary for salvation. Its conclusion is that this sign is not necessary. This teaching continued to be relevant in the Reformation as the Protestants challenged the teaching that the sacraments, or signs of faith, were necessary for salvation or actually gave salvation. The Protestants were returning to the teaching of the first council. Emerson reduces historic Christianity to tradition and dismisses both:

> The second defect of the traditionary and limited way of using the mind of Christ is a consequence of the first; this, namely; that the Moral Nature, that Law of laws whose revelations introduce greatness – yea, God himself – into the open soul, is not explored as the foundation of the established teaching in society. Men have come to speak of the revelation as somewhat long ago given and done, as if God were dead.[11]

Emerson's rejection of tradition is total in that he is not rejecting a particular doctrine of historic Christianity as the Arminians reject the sovereignty of God. Instead, he is rejecting the distinction between God the Creator and humans as the creation. Humans are divine. This is not in the sense that Christianity teaches that humans are made in the image of God. That teaching says humans are *created* in the image of God and, therefore, remain a creation. The image of God is understood in the larger and narrower senses. Where God is infinite, eternal, and unchanging in being, wisdom, power, holiness, goodness, justice, and truth, humans are finite, temporal, and changeable in being, wisdom, power, holiness, goodness, justice, and truth. There remain the incommunicable attributes of infinitude, eternality, and unchangeability that cannot be part of the nature of a created being. But there are the attributes of being, wisdom, power, holiness, goodness, wisdom, and truth that humans share with God although in a finite, temporal, and changeable way. Similarly, there are the attributes of knowledge, holiness, and righteousness. God has these perfectly. All humans share in these formally. However, the unbeliever does not actually have knowledge, holiness, or righteousness.

What Emerson rejects is both the distinction between God and the creation and also the need for a mediator in Christ. Like Paine, who we saw in a previous chapter rejected the need for atonement and Christ, so, too, does Emerson: "Let me admonish you, first of all, to go alone; to refuse the good models, even those which are sacred in the imaginations of men, and dare to love God without mediator or veil."[12]

Just like with Thomas Paine, we see in Emerson the claim that he has correctly understood God, whereas the Christian scriptures are imperfect and contain errors. In both cases, there is no discussion of general revelation except that both Paine and Emerson believe they have grasped what can be known of God, either in Paine's deism or in Emerson's monism.

> The Hebrew and Greek Scriptures contain immortal sentences that have been bread of life to millions. But they have no special integrity; are fragmentary; are not shown in their order to the intellect. I look for the new Teacher that shall follow so far those shining laws that he shall see them come full circle; shall see their rounding completes grace; shall see the world to be the mirror of the soul; shall see the identity of the law of gravitation with purity of heart;

> and shall show that the Ought, that Duty, is one thing with Science, with Beauty, and with Joy.[13]

Although Emerson was influenced by Eastern thought, he also connects it to the teaching of Immanuel Kant. Kant is known for having responded to the skepticism of David Hume. Hume followed the empiricism of John Locke to skeptical conclusions that many found difficult to accept. Kant claimed that Hume's philosophy woke him from his dogmatic slumbers in rationalism, and the philosophy that Kant is known for was an attempt to explain how knowledge is possible. The way he did this was by claiming that although knowledge is from experience, all human experience is shaped by transcendental categories necessary for thought. These transcendentals are not themselves derived from experience. Human knowledge is limited to what can be experienced, and so Kant distinguished between the phenomenon of experience and the noumenal world of being in itself, which can never be known directly. Emerson connected his Transcendentalist school to Kant's teaching:

> It is well known to most of my audience that the Idealism of the present day acquired the name of Transcendental from the use of that term by Immanuel Kant, of Königsberg, who replied to the skeptical philosophy of Locke, which insisted that there was nothing in the intellect which was not previously in the experience of the senses, by showing that there was a very important class of ideas or imperative forms, which did not come by experience, but through the Transcendental. Although, as we have said, there is no pure Transcendentalist, yet the tendency to respect the intuitions and to give them, at least in our creed, all authority over our experience, has deeply colored the conversation and poetry of the present day; and the history of genius and of religion in these times, though impure, and as yet not incarnated in any powerful individual, will be the history of this tendency.[14]

Whereas Kant said that nothing can be known of the noumenal realm since it is beyond all experience, Emerson and other transcendentalists tend to speak a great deal about this and often identify it with the divine or being itself. Even Kant could not keep from speaking about the noumenal and relied on it as the source of the freedom of the will since it is beyond the category of causation.

Emerson uses the same kind of arguments that David Hume used to justify skepticism from the edifice of empiricism: "But ask him why he believes that an uniform experience will continue uniform, or on what grounds he founds his faith in his figures, and he will perceive that his mental fabric is built up on just as strange and quaking foundations as his proud edifice of stone."[15] Emerson rejected the earlier movements of the Enlightenment that he saw as materialistic and reductionistic. The attempt to reduce the good to a pleasure/pain calculus was a mistake. The attempt to reduce the human consciousness to the material world or to experiences of the material world was also a mistake.

> He felt that the spiritual and intellectual biases of the seventeenth and eighteenth centuries, of the Age of Reason, however creative they might have been in their prime, had ended in sterility and denudation, and that the time had come for the reassertion of older wisdoms – still more, for the utterance of fresher ones. On the deepest level he was persuaded that the religious life had been impoverished and all but destroyed, partly by the empty traditionalism of the churches, partly by the dehydrated rationality of the Deists. He had ceased to believe, moreover, in that conception of knowledge and the role of the mind formulated by Lockean empiricism … the image of the world, of nature, that had been so dear to the imagination of the older materialists and mechanists – the image of a World Machine as beautifully, as delicately, constructed as a watch or an orrery, but quite as mechanical – had come to seem to Emerson, as to Goethe and Wordsworth, intolerable. In the sphere of morals, too, he was in full rebellion against the eighteenth century – against that calculus of pleasures and pains which it had made the test of right and wrong.[16]

All knowledge claims from experience are, according to Emerson, resting on this same mistaken foundation. By way of contrast, Emerson builds an alternative foundation on intuition about the divine in all things. "I am nothing; I see all; the currents of the Universal Being circulate through me; I am part or particle of God."[17] And: "Man is conscious of a universal soul within or behind his individual life, wherein, as in a firmament, the natures of Justice, Truth, Love, Freedom, arise and shine. This universal soul, he calls Reason: it is not mine, or thine, or his, but we are its; we are its property and men."[18]

Emerson says that knowing whether our senses teach us about a real material world does not matter. The transcendental or ideal knowledge is all that matters, and the appearances given to us by our senses can be understood to tell us about that without our needing to know whether the material world exists in itself:

> A noble doubt perpetually suggests itself, whether this end be not the Final Cause of the Universe; and whether nature outwardly exists. It is a sufficient account of that Appearance we call the World, that God will teach a human mind, and so makes it the receiver of a certain number of congruent sensations, which we call sun and moon, man and woman, house and trade. In my utter impotence to test the authenticity of the report of my senses, to know whether the impressions they make on me correspond with outlying objects, what difference does it make, whether Orion is up there in heaven, or some god paints the image in the firmament of the soul? The relations of parts and the end of the whole remaining the same, what is the difference, whether land and sea interact, and worlds revolve and intermingle without number or end, – deep yawning under deep, and galaxy balancing galaxy, throughout absolute space, – or, whether, without relations of time and space, the same appearances are inscribed in the constant faith of man? Whether nature enjoy a substantial existence without, or is only in the apocalypse of the mind, it is alike useful and alike venerable to me. Be it what it may, it is ideal to me, so long as I cannot try the accuracy of my senses.[19]

Having argued that the nature of things is consciousness, Emerson then links this to ethics. This follows the formal pattern that ethics presupposes metaphysics. What is good for a being depends on the nature of that being. Following this pattern, Emerson makes claims about the natural law and about the good for humans. "Goodness is by no means merely that which conduces to the multiplication of pleasures or satisfactions: it is 'the adherence in action to the nature of things.' It is, in short, a purely ideal or transcendental conception, and what Emerson repeatedly calls the Moral Law is for him the eternal law of Being itself."[20] Emerson describes it this way: "It has already been illustrated, that every natural process is a version of a moral sentence. The moral law lies at the centre of nature and radiates to the circumference."[21]

> From this transfer of the world into the consciousness, this beholding of all things in the mind, follow easily his whole ethics. It is simpler to be self-dependent. The height, the deity of man is to be self-sustained, to need no gift, no foreign force. Society is good when it does not violate me, but best when it is likest to solitude. Everything real is self-existent. Everything divine shares the self-existence of Deity.[22]

The direct apprehension of beauty is either the good or very close to it. Beauty is apprehended by intuition. The law that Emerson speaks about is related to this understanding of ultimate reality as consciousness, and the good is the direct apprehension of beauty.

> The world thus exists to the soul to satisfy the desire of beauty. This element I call an ultimate end. No reason can be asked or given why the soul seeks beauty. Beauty, in its largest and profoundest sense, is one expression for the universe. God is the all-fair. Truth, and goodness, and beauty, are but different faces of the same All. But beauty in nature is not ultimate. It is the herald of inward and eternal beauty, and is not alone a solid and satisfactory good. It must stand as a part, and not as yet the last or highest expression of the final cause of Nature.[23]

Emerson's description of the natural law rests on his monism – his belief that all is one, that ultimate reality is consciousness, and that all consciousness is part of the divine. This follows the pattern we have seen in moving from epistemology to metaphysics to ethics. His ethical theory, and from that his legal theory, rests on his presuppositions about reality. His reliance on intuition as the highest authority supports his claims about the divine nature of humanity.

> Each creature is only a modification of the other; the likeness in them is more than the difference, and their radical law is one and the same. A rule of one art, or a law of one organization, holds true throughout nature. So intimate is this Unity, that, it is easily seen, it lies under the undermost garment of nature, and betrays its source in Universal Spirit.[24]

From these considerations, we can see that while Emerson used some terminology that was similar to Christianity, he gave these terms new meanings. His belief that all is one and that the human consciousness is divine is pantheism rather than theism. He was an idealist in that he believed that ideas and consciousness were ultimate reality.

> The Emersonian faith is a faith that, without indeed repudiating the whole Judeo-Christian tradition, is no longer specifically either Judaic or Christian. It is purely idealistic belief in an ultimate spiritual reality, an impersonal and timeless Absolute, a transcendent ONE. In its true nature this One is not to be described or defined; it eludes all attempts to confine it in a net of language system; it is simply essential Being – "that Unity, that Over-Soul, within which every man's particular being is contained and made one with all other" – and in its presence all else is only relatively real, is transitional and somehow illusionary … Divinity, as he says, is within as well as above: "God in us worships God." It is this divine principle that is the true self, not "the biographical Ego."[25]

Relying on both Eastern philosophy and his interpretation of Immanuel Kant, Emerson rejected the idea that the mind is passive in attaining knowledge and is instead active in creating reality.

> The philosophy that had given to the mind a dependent and secondary status in its relation to the external world, that had seen it as essentially passive in the process of knowing, that had denied to it an active, a creative role – this philosophy Emerson, like his European precursors, repudiated. What took its place for him was the conviction that the physical world is the *creation* of mind, not its formative context, and that, since mind has somehow brought that world into existence, our knowledge of it is the knowledge the artist has of his own handiwork: "the Intellect builds the universe and is the key to all it contains."[26]

So we see in Emerson a leading and influential example of how the pattern of epistemology, metaphysics, and ethics works out in a worldview. In that sense, he is recapitulating the pattern in the Declaration of Independence. However, he is denying that there is a Creator and, therefore, that humans are created equal. If humans are equal, it is because they are all divine. However, they are not created; they are not creatures in the sense of being finite, temporal, and changeable.

CONCLUSION

We see that this affects his theory of the moral and civil law. Law is a means to the highest good, and the highest good is both self-realization of the self as divine as well as the direct apprehension of beauty. The highest reality is consciousness. The material world is reduced to consciousness. For the individual, there is a movement toward enlightenment where one reaches a consciousness of this highest reality. It is through a kind of direct apprehension or intuition that this takes place. This view of reality and the good has implications for law, both moral and civil.

5 NATURALISM, DARWINISM, THE SELF-EVIDENT, AND LAW

In 1971, the Supreme Court developed the "lemon test." This was used to determine when the government should get involved in matters of religion. It has been used in many contexts, including what it means to teach religion in public schools.

> The Establishment Clause forbids the enactment of any law "respecting an establishment of religion." The Court has applied a three-pronged test to determine whether legislation comports with the Establishment Clause. First, the legislature must have adopted the law with a secular purpose. Second, the statute's principal or primary effect must be one that neither advances nor inhibits religion. Third, the statute must not result in an excessive entanglement of government with religion.[1]

Questions about whether evolution should be taught in public school and if competing theories can be taught alongside it have made their way through both state courts and federal courts. Such instances require defining "science" and "religion." What counts as a religious worldview in contrast to a scientific worldview? When this question is asked, the implication is that "scientific" means "true" or closer to the truth than does "religious," which implies "based on ancient unscientific texts."

The idea of public education is the idea of neutral education. One sect's opinions cannot be promoted over those of others if all are paying for and participating in public education. The state is not involved in establishing one sect over another in public education. However, this is not true where knowledge is concerned. Education is about teaching knowledge. Therefore, the implication is that of philosophical skepticism about the claims of competing sects. Their claims are treated as opinions and not as knowledge.

> The Court has been particularly vigilant in monitoring compliance with the Establishment Clause in elementary and secondary schools. Families entrust public schools with the education of their children, but condition their trust on the understanding that the classroom will not purposely be used to advance religious views that may conflict with the private beliefs of the student and his or her family.[2]

And:

> A governmental intention to promote religion is clear when the State enacts a law to serve a religious purpose. This intention may be evidenced by promotion of religion in general ... If the law was enacted for the purpose of endorsing religion, "no consideration of the second or third criteria [of Lemon] is necessary."[3]

In a case from Louisiana, the Supreme Court decided:

> These same historic and contemporaneous antagonisms between the teachings of certain religious denominations and the teaching of evolution are present in this case. The preeminent purpose of the Louisiana Legislature was clearly to advance the religious viewpoint that a supernatural being created humankind.[4]

The conflict was said to be between the scientific teaching of evolution and the religious teaching of a supernatural being that created humanity.

> The state senator repeatedly stated that scientific evidence supporting his religious views should be included in the public school curriculum to redress the fact that the theory of evolution incidentally coincided with what he characterized as religious beliefs antithetical to his own. The legislation therefore sought to alter the science curriculum to reflect endorsement of a religious view that is antagonistic to the theory of evolution.[5]

The problem was identified as having the aim of endorsing a particular religion:

> In a similar way teaching a variety of scientific theories about the origins of humankind to schoolchildren might be validly done with

> the clear, secular intent of enhancing the effectiveness of science instruction. But because the primary purpose of the Creationism Act is to endorse a particular religious doctrine, the act furthers religion in violation of the Establishment Clause.[6]

The Court decided that belief in God and in creation is inherently religious, while belief in evolution is not. "The doctrine or theory of creation" is commonly defined as "holding that matter, the various forms of life, and the world were created by a transcendent God out of nothing."[7] "'Evolution' is defined as the theory that the various types of animals and plants have their origin in other preexisting types, the distinguishable differences being due to modifications in successive generations."[8] Both of these use basic beliefs to interpret experience. Neither of these basic beliefs is established empirically or through the scientific method. Rather, the philosophical materialism presupposed by evolutionary theory is used to interpret the data and, therefore, is not able to prove the interpretive presupposition (without circular reasoning). Adding belief in God to an otherwise empirical theory makes that theory religious. "Concepts concerning God or a supreme being of some sort are manifestly religious... These concepts do not shed that religiosity merely because they are presented as a philosophy or as a science."[9]

The Louisiana state senator introduced the bill that would teach creation science:

> While a Senate committee was studying scientific creationism, Senator Keith introduced a second draft of the bill, requiring balanced treatment of "evolution science" and "creation science." Although the Keith bill prohibited "instruction in any religious doctrine or materials," it defined "creation science" to include the scientific evidences and related inferences that indicate (a) sudden creation of the universe, energy, and life from nothing; (b) the insufficiency of mutation and natural selection in bringing about development of all living kinds from a single organism; (c) changes only within fixed limits or originally created kinds of plants and animals; (d) separate ancestry for man and apes; (e) explanation of the earth's geology by catastrophism, including the occurrence of a worldwide flood; and (f) a relatively recent inception of the earth and living kinds.[10]

The Court added that the Founding Fathers believed that there is a God: "The fact that the Founding Fathers believed devotedly that there was a God and that the unalienable rights of man were rooted in Him is clearly evidenced in their writings, from the Mayflower Compact to the Constitution itself."[11] But they also saw that this is an inherently religious concept: "Creation '*ex nihilo*' means creation 'from nothing,' and has been found to be an 'inherently religious concept.'"[12]

The Court identified *creation ex nihilo* as a form of Western religion and claimed that there is no rational or evidentiary support for it:

> The argument that creation from nothing in [of the substantially similar Arkansas Balanced Treatment Act] does not involve a supernatural deity has no evidentiary or rational support. To the contrary, "creation out of nothing" is a concept unique to Western religions. In traditional Western religious thought, the conception of a creator of the world is a conception of God. Indeed, creation of the world "out of nothing" is the ultimate religious statement, because God is the only actor.[13]

This means that the Court accepts as "scientific" philosophical materialism but rejects as without proof theism, God the creator, and creation *ex nihilo*. By putting theism into the category of one religion among many, it then takes the position that this is one opinion among others, and all opinions are on equal footing; none of them counts as knowledge.

> Our country has become strikingly multireligious, as well as multiracial and multiethnic. This fact, perhaps more than anything one could write, demonstrates the wisdom of including the Establishment Clause in the First Amendment. States' proposals for what became the Establishment Clause evidence the goal of accommodating competing religious beliefs.[14]

The alternative to this is to recognize the role that basic beliefs play. This is true both for philosophical materialism's claims that only the material world exists and that all events must be interpreted as having material causes. This is not a neutral position. As such, if public education is to be neutral, it cannot teach one basic belief as neutral while rejecting others as somehow not neutral. Education involves interpretation. We use basic beliefs to interpret experience. Therefore, education is not neutral because interpretations presuppose basic beliefs.

PHILOSOPHICAL MATERIALISM AND NATURALISM

We are going to consider how the philosophical materialism and its interpretation of Earth's history and the origin of life came to play a prominent role in American thought.

> The student must bear in mind that the lines of thought here represented were worked out in a society of which a large group, mostly of solid and respectable citizens, had persuaded themselves that the true meaning of Darwinism was an infinite and eternal power of God operating through nature up to man. Armed with that conviction, they were as little touched by the harshness of Sumner as by the humanitarianism of George and Ward; by the same token, they were obtuse to the questions raised by Peirce and James, were dumbly amazed by Holmes, indifferent to the Adamses, and outraged by Veblen (if they so much as noticed him) and by Brandeis (who forced them to pay him attention). They rested relatively secure in the belief that the brutality and waste of the process were minor episodes, and that these were justified by the emergence of the end product, the decent, moral man.[15]

Some American thinkers saw in this a kind of theology, rather than atheism, that fit more with their view of God and their understanding of American history as the emergence of the individual. For instance, "He [Asa Gray], was the first to argue that, far from rushing into atheism, Darwinism established the proof of design in the universe by separating that proof from the no longer tenable hypothesis of the immutability and isolated creation of species."[16] None of this was empirical science as articulated by Francis Bacon or exemplified by Isaac Newton. It was instead a shift in presuppositions about basic questions and an application of these to the interpretation of data. For Americans at the time, this held a particular appeal:

> One reason for the immense appeal of idealism to Americans – especially to the cultivated classes – was that it did supply a methodology for resisting the threat to traditional morality, to the very

> conception of humanity, emanating from *The Origin of Species*. Idealism advertised itself as better equipped for the task than dogmatic theology, Catholic or Protestant, because it could incorporate evolution itself into an ideal scheme, and so enlist it on the side of righteousness, without having to thunder hysterical anathemas. If the Absolute is seen as reproducing Himself through man in the form of an aspiration to perfection, and if prophets of the Absolute can prove even out of Darwin that the discipline of life calls for a "thwarting" of baser impulses, then the process of evolution can be shown (after the first shock is over) to be nothing more than a crude version of the ideal. Hence Idealists could still insist that the spiritual categories – the transcendent forms of the mind – are not the results of evolution, but that the laws of evolution are concepts imposed upon nature by these same spiritual or mental powers. Idealists were prepared – as theologians were not – to turn to pious and moral ends Darwin's blasting of the doctrine of eternally fixed species. Thus they managed to declare that, in spite of Darwin, man is man, the most exalted being in the scale of being, not the miserable and accidental consequence of a haphazard squabble.[17]

This was a kind of appeal to common sense. But what counted as common sense had shifted. The ambiguity of "common sense" was exposed in this shift. What Darwin found to be common sense was not what earlier theologians in the American protestant tradition had relied upon. Instead, it was an import of ideas from German philosophy that better accorded with how thinkers like Darwin understood the world. This includes how Darwin understood change through natural processes devoid of the influence of God. No longer was human history understood in terms of God's covenant with man. Natural evil was an original part of the world and not something imposed by God in response to moral evil.

DARWINISM

Darwin correctly observed that God would not have created a world with the kind of natural evil in it that we observe. But rather than remaining consistent with the Christian answer that God did not create the world with natural evil and that the world was originally very good (without evil), Darwin assumed that there had always been natural evil and, therefore, natural laws, instead of the work of God, must account for the changes and forms of life we see. The other answer, that natural evil was imposed after moral evil and was not original, cannot be disproven through empirical data. Instead, Darwin accepted his answer as a matter of common sense or rationalism. This answer to basic questions permeated all of American thought after this time.

> Both America and England absorbed during the nineteenth century two separate "Germanic invasions." The first came in the form of literature – poetry, drama, and especially of "romance" – with some metaphysical trimmings; it worked mainly upon poets and popularizers, Coleridge and Carlyle in England, Emerson and Theodore Parker in America, but to the mass of citizens, as also to those whom the masses regarded as their sort of philosophers, this Germanism seemed too fantastic to be taken seriously, except as it corrupted aesthetics. The second invasion came armed with a dialectic, a severe discipline, a rationale of history, and a technique of disputation powerful enough to shatter all opposition. One should further emphasize that this version of the German genius gloried in being no anarchy of the motions but a solid conservatism. The support which a righteous America had formerly received from Scottish Realism was now promised in a much more invincible form by this massive Idealism – even though, in order to appropriate it, the American mind had to master a more precise and infinitely subtler kind of reasoning than any for which it had hitherto (except possibly among Puritan theologians) shown the slightest aptitude.[18]

It is worth considering passages from Darwin in which he explains and attempts to justify his approach. Notable in these passages is the reality that they are not empirical and, thus, not scientific. Instead, he argues from his own ideas of how God would have worked in the world. His arguments assume that there has always been natural evil and assume uniformitarianism. This is the belief that the world as we now see it has always been as it is now and that all changes in the past must be explained by currently observed forces. This projects into the past a great expanse of time, because the current forces would require such time to produce the geological and biological realities now observed. He rejects the providential work of God in history, including that there was any interruption, such as the worldwide Flood, to the continued progress of natural history:

> Authors of the highest eminence seem to be fully satisfied with the view that each species has been independently created. To my mind it accords better with what we know of the laws impressed on matter by the Creator, that the production and extinction of the past and present inhabitants of the world should have been due to secondary causes, like those determining the birth and death of the individual. When I view all beings not as special creations, but as the lineal descendants of some few beings which lived long before the first bed of the Silurian system was deposited, they seem to me to become ennobled. Judging from the past, we may safely infer that not one living species will transmit its unaltered likeness to a distant futurity. And of the species now living very few will transmit progeny of any kind to a far distant futurity; for the manner in which all organic beings are grouped, shows that the greater number of species of each genus, and all the species of many genera, have left no descendants, but have become utterly extinct. We can so far take a prophetic glance into futurity as to foretell that it will be the common and widely-spread species, belonging to the larger and dominant groups, which will ultimately prevail and procreate new and dominant species. As all the living forms of life are the lineal descendants of those which lived long before the Silurian epoch, we may feel certain that the ordinary succession by generation has never once been broken, and that no cataclysm has desolated the whole world. Hence we may look with some confidence to a secure future of equally inappreciable length.[19]

The struggle for life and natural selection as aspects of natural evil are understood by Darwin to be original and inherent to the world process. He borrows from Hegelianism the process of conflict that produces world history. The war of nature has always been a part of the creation and is the explanation for what we now see. He says:

> And as natural selection works solely by and for the good of each being, all corporeal and mental endowments will tend to progress towards perfection. It is interesting to contemplate an entangled bank, clothed with many plants of many kinds, with birds singing on the bushes, with various insects flitting about, and with worms crawling through the damp earth, and to reflect that these

> elaborately constructed forms, so different from each other, and dependent on each other in so complex a manner, have all been produced by laws acting around us. These laws, taken in the largest sense, being Growth with Reproduction; Inheritance which is almost implied by reproduction; Variability from the indirect and direct action of the external conditions of life, and from use and disuse; a Ratio of Increase so high as to lead to a Struggle for Life, and as a consequence to Natural Selection, entailing Divergence of Character and the Extinction of less-improved forms. Thus, from the war of nature, from famine and death, the most exalted object which we are capable of conceiving, namely, the production of the higher animals, directly follows. There is grandeur in this view of life, with its several powers, having been originally breathed into a few forms or into one; and that, whilst this planet has gone cycling on according to the fixed law of gravity, from so simple a beginning endless forms most beautiful and most wonderful have been, and are being, evolved.[20]

Darwinism produced a paradigm shift in thinking. This includes but is not limited to what counts as scientific thought. The data he collected indicated microevolution within species that explained diversity in the given species. It did not show macromutation in which one species turns into another that is different in kind. In order to get to that, he had to assume that the microevolutions he saw would eventually produce that kind of change. He had to assume that the fossil record would eventually be filled in and show the gradual steps between each species. This prediction did not come true. The search for these steps in the fossil record continues. But that is not sufficient to falsify Darwinism, because it is not essentially empirical. It rests on presuppositions about how the material world changes and that this is the best explanation of what we experience. To answer how far he would extend his explanation, he says:

> It may be asked how far I extend the doctrine of the modification of species. The question is difficult to answer, because the more distinct the forms are which we may consider, by so much the arguments fall away in force. But some arguments of the greatest weight extend very far. All the members of whole classes can be connected together by chains of affinities, and all can be classified on the same principle, in groups subordinate

> to groups. Fossil remains sometimes tend to fill up very wide intervals between existing orders. Organs in a rudimentary condition plainly show that an early progenitor had the organ in a fully developed state; and this in some instances necessarily implies an enormous amount of modification in the descendants. Throughout whole classes various structures are formed on the same pattern, and at an embryonic age the species closely resemble each other. Therefore I cannot doubt that the theory of descent with modification embraces all the members of the same class. I believe that animals have descended from at most only four or five progenitors, and plants from an equal or lesser number. Analogy would lead me one step further, namely, to the belief that all animals and plants have descended from some one prototype. But analogy may be a deceitful guide. . . Therefore I should infer from analogy that probably all the organic beings which have ever lived on this earth have descended from some one primordial form, into which life was first breathed.[21]

Darwin correctly saw that his system would open up new fields of study for others who wanted to apply naturalism to give explanations of various parts of the world. He thought of this in terms of biology:

> The other and more general departments of natural history will rise greatly in interest. The terms used by naturalists of affinity, relationship, community of type, paternity, morphology, adaptive characters, rudimentary and aborted organs, etc., will cease to be metaphorical, and will have a plain signification. When we no longer look at an organic being as a savage looks at a ship, as at something wholly beyond his comprehension; when we regard every production of nature as one which has had a history; when we contemplate every complex structure and instinct as the summing up of many contrivances, each useful to the possessor, nearly in the same way as when we look at any great mechanical invention as the summing up of the labour, the experience, the reason, and even the blunders of numerous workmen; when we thus view each organic being, how far more interesting, I speak from experience, will the study of natural history become! A grand and almost untrodden field of inquiry will be opened, on the causes and laws of variation, on correlation of growth, on the effects of use and disuse, on the direct action of external conditions, and so forth. The study of domestic productions will rise immensely in value.[22]

However, others eagerly applied this naturalism to fields such as economics, psychology, and law. As is true of any worldview, there was the desire to be total in giving an explanation of reality. The internal coherence of the naturalist's worldview could be augmented and refined. However, the basic beliefs on which it rests are what counts. If these are not true, then the system, however internally consistent, cannot be true.

These long quotes from Darwin are important to help us see how he explained his system and justified his presuppositions. Darwinism flatly rejected the claims of the Declaration of Independence about God and man. In its place, it proposed another kind of natural religion. Similarly, Darwinism rejected Christianity as found in the Westminster Confession of Faith and the leading American theologians. The story of science and religion has been told from many different perspectives. Some theologians felt the pressure to confirm their theological beliefs to this new naturalism that took the name of science. Others, like Charles Hodge of Princeton Seminary, were more conscious of the difference in presuppositions and worked to show how Darwinism represented a new system that was logically incompatible with Christian theism.

The metaphysics of Darwinism fits into the monism of Emerson that we studied earlier. However, it fit better than did Emerson with Hegelian dialectic philosophy. The process of change in history was understood as a result of conflict between a thesis and antithesis that produced a synthesis. Although Darwin speaks about a creator who initially made life, the process that gives us the various species we see today is one of conflict and struggle. In Darwin's view, God did not create the world *very good*, without evil, but instead evil, as natural evil, has been present from the beginning. Taking this as a given, Darwin's theory explains how natural evil has produced the world we see today. Since this struggle does not happen during observations available in a lifetime, great expanses of time are necessary and, therefore, the world's age is adjusted to fit the needed time frame. In this sense Darwinism challenges many of the current trends in American thinking:

> To this cluster of ideas animating the mid-century American mind Darwinism posed a massive challenge. It confounded with a stern biological determinism the nineteenth century's hard-won

> affirmation of moral freedom. It destroyed the traditional reliance of orthodox religion on the works of nature as evidence of the hand of God. It destroyed, just as surely, the transcendentalists' conduit of divinity. For the benevolent, spirit-impregnated nature of the transcendental vision it substituted an iron maiden presiding over endless panoramas of anguish and extinction. The serene cosmic pattern was replaced by the blind movement of mindless forces eternally sifting and shaping all living things, men as well as the lowliest mollusk, towards ends unperceived and perhaps nonexistent. Assaulting the optimistic democratic faith in the worth of the individual, Darwinism disclosed a slaughter of the innocents sanctioned, as it seemed, by a nature concerned with the preservation not of the individual but of the type.[23]

Darwinism presents his theory as a rationalist. It must be true because it fits with his metaphysical presuppositions. The evidence he puts forward can be interpreted in other ways, but these are not acceptable because they rely on metaphysical positions Darwin rejects. Darwin noted at the time of writing that the fossil record did not support his theory but that new discoveries would fill in the blanks. Those blanks remain. However, the faith of a rationalist is such that no lack of evidence can overturn a theory. Nor can evidence to the contrary. The continued attempt to reduce the human mind to the brain as an evolved organ of the human nervous system has not produced results. "The claim that the human mind is the product of evolution is *not* unassailable fact. It is barely coherent."[24]

DARWINISM AND SCIENCE

Darwin's theory came to be championed as "scientific," and this was enough to make intellectuals rally around it.

> The effort by Darwinian biologists to promote Darwin is simply explained. Within the English-speaking world, Darwin's theory of evolution remains the only scientific theory to be widely championed by the scientific community and widely disbelieved by everyone else. No matter the effort made by biologists, the thing continues to elicit the same reaction it has always elicited: You've

> got to be kidding me, right? There is wide appreciation of the fact that if biologists are wrong about Darwin, they are wrong about life, and if they are wrong about life, they are wrong about everything else.[25]

As we saw above in court cases about teaching Darwinism in public schools, it is permitted because it is considered science. Belief in God the Creator is considered religion. However, Darwinism itself rests on claims about God. Darwin speaks about God creating life and that God would not have made the world as we now see it. These are as religious as are the alternative claims about creationism. In other words, one set of presuppositions about God cannot be said to be more "scientific" than another or to be more neutral than another. Metaphysical presuppositions are used to interpret experience and, therefore, are not the outcome of experience. Challenges to the presuppositions of Darwinism are dismissed as backward and prescientific, and yet they persist:

> Suspicions about Darwin's theory arise for two reasons. The first: the theory makes little sense. The second: it is supported by little evidence. In his very long posthumous treatise, *The Structure of Evolutionary Theory*, Stephen Jay Gould explained "the bare bones" of natural selection in this way: "Organisms enjoying differential reproductive success will, on average, be those variants that are fortuitously better adapted to changing local environments." Those variants that are "better adapted" are, of course, precisely those "enjoying differential reproductive success." What else could they be? Biologists believe that tautologies play an unsuspected role in scientific thought and are for this reason worthy of respect. Of course they do. As one might expect, a theory whose assumptions are empty may be widely confirmed by evidence whose relevance is negligible.[26]

Attempts to show that Darwinism is "scientific" require showing how its claims can be falsified. The process of speciation involves a subgroup being geographically isolated from others in its species, and in that context, new adaptations emerge until the group is no longer part of the original species. The fossil record is said to bear this out. And yet such predictions are not found to be the case. There are geological barriers that do not produce new species, and there are multiple explanations of the fossil record:

> But no *theory* has been confirmed since every possibility has been justified. Speciation proceeds in the presence of geographical barriers, and it proceeds in their absence. The demand that the facts somehow support the theory may thus be treated as it so often is in Darwinian thought, and that is as an inconvenience ... The fossil record may be used to justify virtually any position, and often is. There are long eras in which nothing happens. The fire alarms of change then go off in the night. A detailed and continuous record of transition between *species* is missing, those neat sedimentary layers, as Gould noted time and again, never revealing precisely the phenomena that Darwin proposed to explain.[27]

All of this is to say that the driving force of Darwinism is a set of metaphysical presuppositions that came to be adopted as the way to understand the world by intellectuals who rejected historic Christianity. Many at Christian universities were led to believe that if they did not modify their beliefs to reflect Darwinism, they were on the wrong side of a conflict with science itself. Few recognized the metaphysical assumptions behind Darwinism that kept it from being a scientific theory. "Although Darwin depicted natural selection as a force 'daily and hourly scrutinizing' the biological world – a description that would equally designate the activities of the Holy Ghost – efforts to *measure* natural selection have been remarkably unforthcoming."[28]

> If Darwin's theory of evolution has little to contribute to the content of the science, it has much to offer their ideology. It serves as the creation myth of our time, assigning properties to nature previously assigned to God. It thus demands an especially ardent form of advocacy ... Although Darwin's theory is very often compared favorably to the great theories of mathematical physics on the grounds that evolution is as well established as gravity, very few physicists have been heard observing that gravity is as well established as evolution. They know better and they are not stupid.[29]

The tendency in this worldview was to believe that the universe is eternal or without beginning. Although Darwin makes mention of the Creator, the role of the Creator was of little significance and could be dismissed by later thinkers. Whereas Emerson was an idealist, Darwinism gave new energy to philosophical materialism. This is the belief that all of reality can be explained in material terms and that matter has always existed. It continued to be the influential view in twentieth-century science. "Let us suppose, then, that the universe passes sedately from the everlasting to the everlasting. It has been there forever and it will be there forever. This is the universe that Einstein championed before he appreciated the explosive nature of Big Bang cosmology, and it is a universe that has always induced a sense of calm in those who contemplate it."[30]

Indeed, Einstein seems to have hoped that his work would result in a proof that the material world was without beginning:

> The field equation that Einstein introduced in 1915 is a majestic identifier in which curvature, on the one side, and mass, on the other, are placed in the balance and found equal. Einstein had hoped that the equations of general relativity would determine a single world model, and like virtually every other physicist, he believed that his cosmic blueprint would reveal a universe that had neither beginning nor end. Searching for what he wished to find, Einstein discovered a solution to his own equations that specified just such a universe, the great thing having been there from the infinite past and destined to be there into the infinite future. For reasons that he could never make clear, Einstein found a universe so conceived particularly satisfying. Friends of his who knew him well have suggested (to me) that to the end of his life, Einstein regarded an expanding universe with a certain fastidious distaste.[31]

APPLYING DARWIN

Darwinism's implications for morality and law were quickly seen. Humans were no longer understood to have been created equal but were instead the outcome of a struggle for survival that produced inequalities. These inequalities bore the strength of an *is* rather than of an *ought*. While people might feel that there ought not to be inequalities, Darwinism explained why these are the case and were bolstered by the supposed fact that these inequalities were scientifically explained. Morality was made to fit into this model:

> Like so many other positions, moral relativism has been promoted from the back of the classroom to the podium. "The West," the

> philosopher Richard Rorty writes, "has cobbled together, in the course of the last two hundred years, a specifically secularist moral tradition – one that regards the free consensus of the citizens of a democratic society, rather than the Divine Will, as the source of moral imperatives." The words *free consensus*, although sonorous, come to nothing more than the declaration that just so long as there is rough agreement within society, what its leaders say goes. This was certainly true of Nazi Germany.[32]

The idea that a majority somehow guarantees or defines the truth is a form of philosophical skepticism. The idea is that since we cannot actually have knowledge, the alternative is that the majority decides how to rule, although protections should be put in place for the minority position. This strategy fits into the idea that factions are a necessary or unavoidable part of human life in society. The majority factions rule while protecting the rights of the minority factions. Darwinism introduced a new idea into this equation with the idea that the tension between these factions produced a synthesis and then a new conflict. All of this was aimed at the supposed survival or evolution of the species.

In this intellectual history, the phrase "free thinkers" came to refer to those persons who did not accept tradition but instead worked out their own worldview. What this actually resulted in was philosophical materialism. Tradition was rejected as a kind of perpetual acceptance of what is irrational and meaningless. In its place, philosophical materialism was understood to be the best philosophical position. Of course, philosophical materialism is one of the oldest philosophies, dating to the early Greek philosophers. In this sense, it also is a tradition. The moral philosophy of materialism was the promotion of happiness:

> While I am opposed to all orthodox creeds, I have a creed myself; and my creed is this. Happiness is the only good. The time to be happy is now. The place to be happy is here. The way to be happy is to make others so. This creed is somewhat short, but it is long enough for this life, strong enough for this world. If there is another world, when we get there we can make another creed.[33]

Free thinkers were eager to enlist notable Americans into their ranks. If free thinking merely means thinking for oneself, it is not in tension with accepting historic Christianity. A person can examine the evidence and come to the conclusion that God created and that there is a need for vicarious atonement. However, free thinking did not mean this. Instead, it meant accepting skepticism, which is the view that we cannot actually have knowledge. As such, it claimed important Founding Fathers as among free thinkers:

> The only freethinkers who have received their due in American history are Thomas Jefferson and James Madison, in spite of the fact that they were denigrated by their Calvinistic contemporaries as atheists, heretics, and infidels (then understood in its literal, original sense – *unfaithful ones*). It is impossible to consign former presidents or the authors of the nation's secular scriptures to a historical limbo.[34]

Free Thought defined itself in contrast to historic Christianity. An important part of this was defining all of religions as superstition and philosophical materialism as science. Although materialism is preempirical in that it is used to interpret experience and, therefore, cannot be the conclusion of experience, it was advanced as more "modern" than superstition that referred to the existence of a nonmaterial being. This explains both the decline of Emerson's idealism as well as a decline in the theistic understanding of science. Theism and science were purported to be adversaries.

> American freethought derived much of its power from an inclusiveness that encompassed many forms of rationalist belief. Often defined as a total absence of faith in God, freethought can better be understood as a phenomenon running the gamut from the truly antireligious – those who regarded all religion as a form of superstition and wished to reduce its influence in every aspect of society – to those who adhered to a private, unconventional faith revering some form of God or Providence but at odds with orthodox religious authority. American freethinkers included deists, who, like many of the founding fathers, believed in a "watchmaker God" who set the universe in motion but subsequently took no active role in the affairs of men; agnostics; and unabashed atheists. What many types of freethinkers shared, regardless of their views on the existence or nonexistence of a divinity, was a rationalistic approach to fundamental questions of earthly existence – a conviction that the affairs of human beings should be governed not by

faith in the supernatural but by a reliance on reason and evidence adduced from the natural world. It was this conviction, rooted in the Enlightenment philosophy, that carried the day when the former revolutionaries gathered in Philadelphia in 1787 to write the Constitution.[35]

DARWIN AND THE INTELLECTUALS

American intellectuals were quick to adopt Darwinism and to draw out its implications for morality and the highest good. Understanding the good as happiness, these thinkers explained how happiness is best attained through the Darwinian process. Happiness was understood as individual pleasure that could be maximized through the Darwinian explanation of biology. Josiah Royce, in his work "The Problem of Job," worked to explain how suffering was not incompatible with the highest good. His understanding of Job was divorced from the actual text in which Job comes to a greater understanding of God. In the Book of Job, Job is described as the most blameless man. However, this does not mean that he is sinless. Through the process of suffering, Job at the end claims that he has come to see God. However, Royce gives the story a much different meaning:

> The knowing of the good, in the higher sense, depends upon contemplating the overcoming and subordination of a less significant impulse, which survives even in order that it should be subordinated. Now this law, this form of the knowledge of the good, applies as well to the existence of moral as to that of sensuous ill. If moral evil were simply destroyed and wiped away from the external world, the knowledge of moral goodness would also be destroyed ... What is needed, then, for the definition of the divine knowledge of a world that in its wholeness is perfect, is not a divine knowledge that shall ignore, wipe out and utterly make naught the existence of any ill, whether physical or moral, but a divine knowledge to which shall be present that love of the world as a whole which is fulfilled in the endurance of physical ill, in the subordination of moral ill, in the thwarting of impulses which survive even when subordinated, in the acceptance of repugnancies which are still eternal, in the triumph over an enemy that endures even

> through its eternal defeat, and in the discovery that the endless tension of the finite world is included in the contemplative consciousness to the repose and harmony of eternity.[36]

Those who wanted to incorporate God into their new theory relied on a synthesis of Emerson and Darwin. God was understood to be the idealistic reality that explains the rest of being. Josiah Royce said, "To view God's nature thus is to view his nature as the whole idealistic theory views him, not as the Infinite One beyond the finite imperfections, but as the being whose unity determines the very constitution, the lack, the tension, and relative disharmony of the finite world."[37] Evil is, therefore, a necessary part of the world. In contrast to the theistic claim that God created the world very good, Royce explained evil as a necessary aspect of the world. "The existence of evil, then, is not only consistent with the perfection of the universe, but is necessary for the very existence of that perfection."[38]

One of the persistent problems for Darwin's theory was to explain the human mind. Chauncy Wright reduced the human mind to language and sought to explain how language could develop through the slow evolutionary process:

> Language, strictly so called, which some of these animals also have, or signs *purposely* used for communication, is not only required for scientific knowledge, but a second step of generalization is needed, and is made through reflection, by which this use of a sign is itself made an object of attention, and the sign is recognized in its general relations to what it signifies, and to what it has signified in the past, and will signify in the future. It is highly improbable that such a knowledge of knowledge, or such a *re*-cognition, belongs in any considerable, or effective, degree to even the most intelligent of the lower animals, or even to the lowest of the human race. This is what is properly meant by being "rational" or being a "rational animal."[39]

Interestingly, he contrasts his theory with "special creation" and dismisses this as unscientific. In its place, he proposes a slow, uniformitarian theory of how language developed as the signs of communication by lower animals. These signs eventually developed into what we now call language:

> It has come to be understood, and very generally allowed, that the conception of the origin of man as an animal race, as well as the origin of individual men within it, in accordance with the continuity of organic development maintained in the theory of evolution, does not involve any very serious difficulties, or difficulties so great as are presented by any other hypothesis of this origin, not excepting that of "special creation"– if that can be properly called a hypothesis, which is, in fact, a resumption of all the difficulties of natural explanation, assuming them to be insuperable and summarizing them under a single positive name. Yet in this evolution, the birth of self-consciousness is still thought by many to be a step not following from antecedent conditions in "nature," except in an incidental manner, or in so far only as "natural" antecedents have prepared the way for the "supernatural" advent of the self-conscious soul."[40]

Chauncy Wright and John Dewey made significant contributions to the adoption of Darwinism into American thinking and education. Wright was part of the Metaphysical Club that included William James and Oliver Wendell Holmes Jr. His work on the evolution of self-consciousness attempted to explain how the human mind can be accounted for by material evolution without reference to a soul or God. His theory of science is as follows:

> In science and in scientific facts there is implied a conscious purpose of including particular facts under general facts, and the less general under the more general ones. Science, in the modern use of the term, consists, essentially, of a knowledge of things and events either as effects of general causes, or as instances of general classes, rules, or laws; or even as isolated facts of which the class, law, rule, or cause is sought. The conscious purpose of arriving at general facts and at an adequate statement of them in language, or of bringing particular facts under explicit general ones, determines for any knowledge a scientific character.[41]

The problem is in distinguishing between facts and interpretation of facts. The facts that Wright starts with are philosophical materialism. This is not an empirical fact but a philosophical presupposition. His entire system will only be true insofar as philosophical materialism is true. This is not a question for empirical science but for philosophy. However, he does not reckon with this and instead moves forward to give a theory of knowledge, language, and the human mind that presupposes his materialism. Language is the use of words to communicate sense images.

> Hence language, in its narrower sense, as the instrument of reflective thought, appears to depend on the intensity of significant, or representative, images; since the power to attend to these and intensify them still further, at the same time that an equivalent outward sign is an object of attention, would appear to depend solely on the relative intensities of the two states, or on the relations of intensity in perception and imagination, or in the original and revived impressions.[42]

He uses this theory of language and the assumption that humans are on a continuum with animals to make claims about differences between humans:

> The inferior and savage races of men, whose languages do not include any abstract terms like truth, goodness, and sweetness, but only concrete ones, like true, good, and sweet, would hardly be able to form a conception, even a vague and obscure one, of the mystic's research of omniscience in the profundities of self-consciousness. They ought on this account, perhaps, to be regarded as races distinct from that of these philosophers, at least mentally; and to be classed, in spite of their powers of speech and limited vocabularies, with the dumb but still intelligent animals.[43]

Human language is more advanced than what is found among animals because humans have larger brains and are, therefore, able to have a larger number of sense experiences.

> This greatest of human qualities, intelligent self-consciousness, understood in its actual and proper limits, would follow as a consequence of a greater brain, a greater or more powerful and vivid memory and imagination, bringing to light, as it were, and into distinct consciousness, phenomena of thought which reflective observation refers to the subject, already known in the dumb animal, or distinguished as an active cause from the forces of outward nature and from the wills of other animals.[44]

However, this does not explain self-consciousness. The ability to reflect on thought itself is not explained in Wright's analysis of language as attachments of words to senses. Self-consciousness is not simply another level of placing words to senses. In this, he seems to be borrowing from David Hume, who said, "when I look inside all I see are a bundle of mental images." The problem for both Wright and Hume is to account for the "I" that is doing the looking. This "I," the self, is not simply the mental images but is the consciousness looking at the mental images. A larger brain might account for more sensations but not for this self who looks at the sensations. Nevertheless, Wright states his empirical presuppositions when he says, "Truths independent of all experience are not known to exist."[45] Wright is an early positivist. Positivists analyze the meaning of a belief only in terms of how it can be empirically verified.

> Is it not to discover the causes, classes, laws, or rules that determine the existence, properties, or production of a thing or event? And when these are discovered, is there any further occasion for inquiry, except in the interest of feelings which would have checked inquiry at the outset?[46]

John Dewey, as one of the American pragmatists, claimed that the truth of a belief could be understood in terms of its usefulness. However, just what counts as useful depends on many other presuppositions. We find in Dewey both an acceptance of Darwinism and philosophical materialism. Therefore, what he finds useful is relative to these philosophical assumptions. He dismisses "metaphysical" study while at the same time having his own metaphysical presuppositions:

> When Henry Sidgwick casually remarked in a letter that as he grew older his interest in what or who made the world was altered into interest in what kind of a world it is anyway, his voicing of a common experience of our own day illustrates also the nature of that intellectual transformation effected by Darwinian logic. Interest shifts from the wholesale essence of special changes back to the question of how special changes serve and defeat concrete purposes; shifts from an intelligence that shaped things once for all to the particular intelligences which things are even now shaping; shifts from an ultimate goal of good to the direct increments of justice and happiness that intelligent administration of existent conditions may beget and that present carelessness or stupidity will destroy or forego.[47]

To know what kind of world this is requires knowing what is real and what is not. He presupposes that the material world alone is real, and that it has existed from eternity, and that change in the world is due to a Hegelian process that can explain the origin of species and even the development of human society. He saw the role of Darwinism as having applied the Hegelian system of change and transition to give a new logic of understanding life. "The influence of Darwin upon philosophy resides in his having conquered the phenomena of life for the principle of transition, and thereby freed the new logic for application to mind and morals and life."[48]

Dewey saw that Darwinism gave an explanation of the world that took away any need for appeals to an intelligent creator. Although he saw this in Darwinism, all this means is that he saw that Darwinism and theism were operating on competing basic beliefs.

> The Darwinian principle of natural selection cut straight under this philosophy. If all organic adaptations are due simply to constant variation and the elimination of those variations which are harmful in the struggle for existence that is brought about by excessive reproduction, there is no call for a prior intelligent causal force to plan and preordain them ... he holds that since variations are in useless as well as useful directions, and since the latter are sifted out simply by the stress of the conditions of struggle for existence, the design argument as applied to living beings is unjustifiable; and its lack of support there deprives it of scientific value as applied to nature in general.[49]

Arguments in favor of the philosophical materialism and Hegelian thought process behind Darwinism were not forthcoming. Instead, the reasons given to support Darwinism were that it made theism unnecessary. This is hardly news. If a nontheistic worldview is true, then theism is not true. However, such an insight, such as it is, does not help us to know which of the two competing beliefs is true. There were other reasons or motivations for wanting theism and the idea of God the creator to lose its influence in American thought.

Although there were notable thinkers at American institutions of higher education that sought to find a compromise between Darwin and theism, the quote from Dewey shows that Darwinism and its logical implications are such that theism is ruled out. Neo-Darwinists and the New Atheists of the twentieth and twenty-first centuries make this point. What we are left to consider is how we can know which competing basic belief is true. If Darwinism is true, then humans are not created equal and are not given rights by their creator.

CONCLUSION

Because Darwinism claims to be scientific, it takes on all of the authority that comes with scientific reasoning. However, the "scientific method" used by Darwinists is not the same as the scientific method explained during the scientific revolution by thinkers like Francis Bacon. Instead, it is the use of philosophical assumptions that are accepted as true perhaps simply because they are nontheistic, and the subsequent construction of a worldview on this foundation.

For our study, this leaves us to consider the role of basic beliefs in forming the foundation of a worldview and what it means to use reason to critically analyze basic beliefs. We have seen that common sense and intuition are used in the place of reason and that the result is skepticism, since neither of these can give certainty. And yet we do not want to abandon reason as the source of certainty or claim that certainty is not possible, because common sense and intuition have failed to provide knowledge. Next we turn to the influence of Charles Finney and the Second Great Awakening on American thinking about God and redemption. This movement occurs just before and then during the time that Darwinism was introduced into American thought.

6 REVIVALISM, NEW RELIGIOUS MOVEMENTS, AND LAW

In the case *Holy Trinity Church v. United States* (1892), the issue was one of whether a church could hire a foreign minister when hiring foreign workers was illegal. The court decided in favor of the church, arguing that Christianity has a special role in the United States. Justice Brewer delivered the opinion of the Court. He said, "But beyond all these matters no purpose of action against religion can be imputed to any legislation, state or national, because this is a religious people. This is historically true."[1] He then gave a history of the United States going all the way back to Columbus. He argued that the purposes of Columbus and of colonists under King James I were religious. He noted the language of the Mayflower Compact, the orders under which the government of Connecticut was established, and the privileges given to William Penn. He also cited the Declaration of Independence as proof of the affirmation that God plays a role in human life.

> If we pass beyond these matters to a view of American life as expressed by its laws, its business, its customs and its society, we find everywhere a clear recognition of the same truth. Among other matters note the following: The form of oath universally prevailing, concluding with an appeal to the Almighty; the custom of opening sessions of all deliberative bodies and most conventions with prayer; the prefatory words of all wills, "In the name of God, amen"; the laws respecting the observance of the Sabbath, with the general cessation of all secular business, and the closing of courts, legislatures, and other similar public assemblies on that day; the churches and church organizations which

> abound in every city, town and hamlet; the multitude of charitable organizations existing everywhere under Christian auspices; the gigantic missionary associations, with general support, and aiming to establish Christian missions in every quarter of the globe.[2]

The idea that the United States is a Christian nation was approached in this case as a historical and sociological matter. It does not address the question of the truth of Christian beliefs or of the relationship between the government and specific religious beliefs. Other cases come closer to doing that. The decade before this case, there had been other cases dealing with Mormonism and polygamy. In these cases, arguments were made about what is necessary for the good and well-ordered society.

In *Reynolds v. United States* (1879), George Reynolds, a secretary to Brigham Young, was appealing his conviction for polygamy. In the decision, the court refers for the first time to the "wall of separation" mentioned by Jefferson in a letter to the Danbury Baptists. The court unanimously decided:

> Congress cannot pass a law for the government of the Territories which shall prohibit the free exercise of religion. The first amendment to the Constitution expressly forbids such legislation... The question to be determined is, whether the law now under consideration comes within this prohibition. The word "religion" is not defined in the Constitution. We must go elsewhere, therefore, to ascertain its meaning, and nowhere more appropriate, we think, than to the history of the times in the midst of which the provision was adopted. The precise point of the inquiry is, what is the religious freedom which has been guaranteed.[3]

Although a strict definition of "religion" was not given, the basis for thinking about religion was one of distinguishing between beliefs or opinions on the one hand and actions on the other. The closest thing to a definition is a quote used from Madison that religion is one's duty owed to the Creator. The court based its ruling on a consideration of religious freedom and the contrast with common law concerning marriage. When opinions interfere with peace and good order, then it is right for the government to get involved. It noted the importance of marriage to the state and, therefore, the government's role in making laws regarding marriage:

> Marriage, while from its very nature a sacred obligation, is nevertheless, in most civilized nations, a civil contract, and usually regulated by law. Upon it society may be said to be built, and out of its fruits spring social relations and social obligations and duties with which the government is necessarily required to deal.[4]

The court concluded that polygamy does interfere with good order and that it introduces a new idea of marriage into the common law:

> The only question which remains, is, whether those who make polygamy a part of their religion are excepted from the operation of the statute ... This would be introducing a new element into criminal law. Laws are made for the government of actions, and while they cannot interfere with mere religious belief and opinions, they may with practices. Suppose one believed that human sacrifices were a necessary part of religious worship, would it be seriously contended that the civil government under which he lived could not interfere to prevent a sacrifice?[5]

The court ruled that there was criminal intent because the issue was not one of ignorance about the law but one of disregarding a known law. The court also distinguished between ignorance of a fact that might mitigate criminal intent and ignorance of the law itself, which is no excuse:

> A criminal intent is generally an element of crime, but every man is presumed to intend the necessary and legitimate consequences of what he knowingly does ... Every act necessary to constitute the crime was knowingly done, and the crime was therefore knowingly committed. Ignorance of a fact may sometimes be taken as evidence of a want of criminal intent, but not ignorance of the law. The only defense of the accused in this case is his belief that the law ought not to have been enacted. It matters not that this belief was a part of his professed religion: it was still belief, and belief only.[6]

The court decided this case on the basis of what a good and well-ordered society requires in terms of actions and institutions like marriage. The truth of beliefs about monogamy and polygamy were, in one sense, set aside, although there are implications in the argument that monogamy is conducive to a well-ordered society and polygamy is not. This highlights on the one hand government attempting to stay out of matters of the truth of religious questions but on the other hand the reality that decisions still have implications about theological and religious matters.

THE SECOND GREAT AWAKENING AND CHARLES FINNEY

The Second Great Awakening unleashed new levels of religious diversity that challenged the American system of law. Not only were new Protestant denominations developed, but new religious movements grew out of the methods of the Awakening. It reached a new level of challenge in its understanding of how to come to knowledge and using this to challenge previous beliefs, about God, salvation, the nature of humans and the church, and the goal of life. In order to highlight how these areas of change occurred and the challenges they presented, we will look at the work and theology of Charles Finney. This will help us understand the new changes in the Protestant world and also how new religious movements used these same ideas to develop new systems.

Although Finney was ordained as a Presbyterian minister, he admitted that he had not read the Westminster Confession of Faith. His neglect of this doctrinal standard turned to a rejection and disdain for the work of the Westminster Assembly in formulating and expressing the theology of the Reformation. He said:

> The Assembly of Divines did more than to assume the necessity of a Pope to give law to the opinions of men; they assumed to create an immortal one, or rather to embalm their own creed, and preserve it as the Pope of all generations; or it is more just to say, that those who have adopted that confession of faith and catechism as an authoritative standard of doctrine, have absurdly adopted the most obnoxious principle of Popery, and elevated their confession and catechism to the Papal throne and into the place of the Holy Ghost. That the instrument framed by that assembly should in the nineteenth century be recognized as the standard of the church, or of an intelligent branch of it, is not only amazing, but I must say that it is most ridiculous. It is as absurd in theology as it would be in any other branch of science, and as injurious and stultifying as

> it is absurd and ridiculous. It is better to have a living than a dead Pope. If we must have an authoritative expounder of the word of God, let us have a living one, so as not to preclude the hope of improvement. "A living dog is better than a dead lion" (Eccl. 9:4), so a living Pope is better than a dead and stereotyped confession of faith, that holds all men bound to subscribe to its unalterable dogmas and its unvarying terminology.[7]

This gives us a look into his view of Christian doctrine, how it is understood, and what is authoritative in Christian belief. Of course, the Divines understood their work to be based on what the scriptures teach and to be an explication of that in response to challenges to the faith. So the issue is not one about the authority of the Bible. Nor is it one of how to respond to new challenges. All of the questions that Finney faced about free will, regeneration, and evangelism were addressed. Nothing new in kind had presented itself. Instead, it is that Finney either did not know what the Confession said or he simply disagreed with it. In disagreeing with it, he would need to be able to state its position and then argue about why it is false and why his view is true. We will look at his defense of his own beliefs about the *ordo salutis*, the order in which salvation is applied. He is said to be distinctively American in his focus on the individual's free will as the focus in salvation.

He introduced new methods into revivalism that he argued worked in a law-like manner to bring about a revival. These "new measures" included a direct presentation of sin and its consequences, public prayers that included the names of clergy who had not supported his work, suspending normal church services and replacing them with lengthy meetings each night that lasted a week or more, and the "anxious bench" set up for people considering accepting the call to repentance that eventually became the altar call.[8]

Finney's *Systematic Theology* was his more mature work that explained his theology and the methods he used in evangelicalism. It justified those methods by giving a theology to support them. Reviewers of the book, like Charles Hodge and Benjamin Warfield, noted that it hardly mentioned the scriptures in its first half and was, instead, better classified as a kind of natural theology. In it, Finney begins with his anthropology, or theory of human nature and human will, and from there develops his account of obligation and free will. After lengthy discussions of these, he gets to the reality of sin and then the role of Christ in salvation. He leaves the main foundational beliefs of Christianity about the nature of God and the knowledge of God undeveloped and mostly untouched. However, his claims about human nature and salvation have implications about the nature of God. His is a kind of voluntarism, a focus on the will as central, both for God and for humans. In contrasting his theology with others, he says: "They seemed to me to resolve all religion into states either of the intellect or of the sensibility, which my consciousness assured me were wholly passive or involuntary."[9] By way of contrast, he believes the successful approach is to look at the active operations of the will abstracted from other elements of human nature such as beliefs and desires that inform what is willed.

Finney viewed himself as providing a schema that would rescue Christianity from its ailments. He believed he had identified the main misunderstandings that needed to be addressed and that by getting these into place, Christians will be able to unite in their work as Christians. In this sense, he had the professed desire to overcome the divisions and disagreements among Christians and thought he had struck on the answer.[10] The actual outcome was more division. As Michael Horton notes:

> Enthusiasm proved to be a more unstable guarantor of unity than theological conviction, as the former is inherently more subjective and individualistic than the latter.... Enthusiasm, not theology, emerged as the agent of discord. While Finney may have objected to a "paper pope" in the Westminster Standards, the nineteenth century created scores of living ones.[11]

Finney begins by diagnosing the problem. It is that religious teachers do not sufficiently understand the laws of knowledge in order to convict their hearers. They do not know the different classes of knowledge and how people come to possess a belief in them. "Consequently they either spend time in worse than useless efforts to prove first or self-evident truths, or expect truths susceptible of demonstration to be received and rested in without such demonstration."[12] Finney occupies himself with the idea of what is self-evident, and we will see how it relates to the claims in the Declaration of Independence. He agrees that there are self-evident truths and expands these beyond those in the Declaration.

Finney begins with the role of reason in affirming beliefs. He defends the role of reason in that if reason deceives us in one thing, it may deceive us in all of the most important questions. If it ever gives false testimony, then reason must be dismissed. And, he says, if we cannot safely appeal to reason, then how can we know what the Bible means? "For it is the faculty by which we get at the truth of the oracles of God."

> If the intelligence affirms it, it must be true, or reason deceives us. But if the reason deceives in this, it may also in other things. If it fails us here, it fails us on the most important of all questions. If reason gives false testimony, we can never know truth from error upon any moral subject. We certainly can never know what religion is or is not if the testimony of reason can be set aside. If the reason cannot be safely appealed to, how are we to know what the Bible means? For it is the faculty by which we get at the truth of the oracles of God.[13]

The tricky point will be to define reason and distinguish it from what Finney or any other author finds *reasonable.* He does this by defining classes of truths. "This class of truths possess all the characteristics of self-evident truths, to wit: they are universal truths; they are necessary truths; they are truths of direct intuition; they are truths of certain knowledge."[14] Following the format of the Declaration of Independence, Finney looks to lay the foundation for his system in what is self-evident. He defines this as intuitive truths, which means those that are directly understood and not in need of proof. They are also universal in that all humans will intuit their truth. And they are certain; they cannot be false. If someone rejects these truths, he says that there can be no further discussion:

> There is no reasoning with one who calls in question the first truths of reason and demands proof of them. All reasoning must, from the nature of mind and the laws of reasoning, assume the first-truths of reason as certain, and admitted, and as the a priori condition of all logical deduction and demonstration. Some one of these must be assumed as true, directly or indirectly, in every syllogism and in every demonstration.[15]

Among the truths that are self-evident, Finney lists "That God and space and duration are infinite, that all God's attributes must be infinite, are self-evident truths of reason; that is, they are truths of a priori affirmation and assumption."[16] It is hard to understand either how these are self-evident or how each of these is infinite in an equivocal sense. To say that God is infinite presupposes that God exists. To say that if God exists as understood in theism, then "God is infinite" is more of a tautology than a self-evident truth. Indeed, he perhaps means that self-evident truths are simply tautologies. But the well-known critique of this view is that such truths tell us nothing about the world itself but only about our use of words.

Finney also takes notice of the fact that many people are not aware of self-evident truths. These truths are assumed by all people in the rest of their thinking even if they are never brought to the conscious mind. They are necessary assumptions for thinking. This is why he could say that there can be no discussion with persons who deny these truths. He explains it this way:

> Suppose, for example, that the law of causality should not be at all times or at any time a subject of distinct thought and attention. Suppose that the proposition in words should never be in the mind, that "every event must have a cause." Still, the truth is there in the form of absolute knowledge, a necessary assumption, an a priori affirmation, and the mind has so firm a hold of it as to be utterly unable to overlook, forget, or practically deny it.[17]

And:

> First truths of reason, then, let it be distinctly remembered, are always and necessarily assumed, though they may be seldom thought of. They are universally known before the words are understood by which they may be expressed; and although they may never be expressed in a formal proposition, yet the mind has as certain a knowledge of them as it has of its own existence.[18]

His description involves three parts that are formally true. (I) What is self-evident is known without proof because it is what is used for proof. (II) Such truths are assumed in all thought and discussion. (III) There can be no common ground when these are denied. However, he runs into problems when he begins to identify these self-evident truths.

For instance, causality. He argues that it is universally assumed by all persons. This might or might not be true. It is well known that Hume denied this and offered criticisms of causation. There are forms of radical empiricism, whether in Buddhism or occasionalism, that deny any causal connections between moments of experience. So it may turn out to be true that causation is a necessary assumption for intelligibility, but it will require a proof, which means that causation is not the most basic level. Causation itself must be understood, and so the most basic level must identify the very laws of thought that allow for understanding.

Finney says something like this when he says, "The laws of logic are inherent in every mind; but in various states of development in different minds."[19] The role of these laws is to support all reasoning, and therefore they cannot themselves be questioned. "All reasoning proceeds upon the assumption of these truths. It must do so of necessity. It is preposterous to attempt to prove first truths to a moral agent; for, being a moral agent, he must absolutely know them already."[20] It is curious that he emphasizes the moral agent rather than simply any thinker. It raises the question as to whether these can be disconnected, as if there could be a thinker who cannot think about what is good. In the last quote, he gives us two reasons for accepting these laws. One is that all reasoning rests on them. The other is that all moral agents absolutely know them already. Since he has already told us that not every person is conscious of these laws, by "absolutely know," he must mean that they presuppose these laws in all of their other thinking and moral activities. He explains, "There are many truths which men, all sane men, certainly know, of which they not only seldom think, but which, in theory, they strenuously deny."[21]

He gives us a taxonomy of these kinds of truths. This is: "The a priori truths of reason may be classed under the heads of first truths: self-evident truths which are necessary and universal: and self-evident truths not necessary and universal."[22] He reiterates that to deny these is to deny what is known most perfectly and what is necessary for knowledge.[23] "It is a very common case, that the unbeliever denies in words, and endeavors to refute in theory, that which he nevertheless assumes as true, in all his practical judgments."[24]

He gives some specific examples of these kinds of truths. They are ontological claims, not epistemological claims, and that is significant. They are: "I have already noticed three of this class, to wit; the truth of causality – the existence of space and of time. That the whole of any thing is equal to all its parts, is also a truth of this class, universally and necessarily known and assumed by every moral agent. Also, that a thing cannot be and not be at the same time."[25] The last is a form of the law of noncontradiction. Finney states it the way Aristotle stated it. In this presentation, it has the meaning of an ontological statement about being. However, as a law of thought, it is formally stated: not both *a* and *non-a* in the same respect and the same time. This law applies both to thought and to being.

Finney recognizes another class of these truths. They are self-evident truths of intuition but are not universal. They include our own existence and personal identity.[26] Finney, like the Declaration of Independence, begins his system with what he states is self-evident. On this basis, he then believes he can build what is a Pelagian system of salvation in which God cooperates with humans in the redemptive process. It will be important for our study to look at his system, because he demonstrates how the term "God," something the Declaration took to be self-evident, has numerous meanings and how competing theories of redemption are rooted in competing theories of the nature of God.

Beginning with the will, Finney denies that there is a fallen will that is unable to accept the redemptive offer of God. "The doctrines of a nature, sinful per se, of a necessitated will, of inability, and of physical regeneration, and physical Divine influence in regeneration, with their kindred and resulting dogmas, embarrassed and even confounded me at every step. I often said to myself, 'If these things are really taught in the Bible, I must be an infidel.'"[27] This is consistent with his rejection of the Westminster Confession and the teachings of the Reformation summarized in that document. But it is also consistent with having misunderstood those doctrines.

Interestingly, Finney accuses his theological opponents of fideism. "I found that the discriminating teachers of religion were driven to confess that they could not establish the logical consistency of their system, and that they were obliged to shut their eyes and believe, when revelation seemed to conflict with the affirmations of reason."[28] This is a bold and unsubstantiated claim, especially in light of the theological work done by the Princeton theologians like Charles Hodge. The Reformed system and its defenders at Princeton were often accused of using reason. Finney simply claims that they do not and instead assert their views blindly. Perhaps the way to explain this is due to his unquestioned assumption that free will requires the ability to do otherwise. He takes this as true without considering the alternative view that a free will is a will that is unhindered, or free to do what is wanted. His entire system of theology begins with the claim that a free will is the ability to do otherwise, and he takes this to its logical conclusions.[29]

On the basis of this view of freedom, he developed his thinking about the moral law and obligation. "What I have said on 'Moral Law' and on the 'Foundation of Moral Obligation' is the key to the whole subject. Whoever masters and understands these can readily understand all the rest."[30] This is the key, because in evangelism, the process begins by getting the audience to understand that they have violated the moral law and stand in a position of guilt before God. He thinks it is only by getting this message understood that the process of a human will accepting the offer of salvation can begin.

The moral law is summarized as universal benevolence. He takes a position in an older debate in American theology. Jonathan Edwards had said that the highest goal was disinterested benevolence for being. Others had said that the highest goal was love of God. In a way, philosophers sought to reconcile these by arguing that if one loves God, one loves God's creation. However, there is also the reality that some things, such as evil and evildoers, are to be hated. Finney states his view this way: "Moral law, as we have seen, requires love, and only love, to God and man, or to God and the universe. This love, as we have seen, is goodwill, choice, the choice of an end, the choice of the highest well-being of God, and of the universe of sentient existences."[31] We can infer a link between his teaching universal love of all human choice and the more liberal forms of Protestantism, some of which trace their beliefs to Finney.

The purpose of God in creating was his own well-being and that of all existence. This well-being is happiness. God created in order to be happy. "His own glory and happiness are infinitely the greatest good in and to the universe."[32]

God's plan for humans, including redemption, is for them to reach the highest happiness. Finney equates happiness and the good. His explanation of Christianity and the offer of salvation is that human happiness depends on accepting this offer. This highest happiness is achieved in heaven after death. The alternative is everlasting misery.

This misery is the consequence of sin. In analyzing the claim that the consequence of sin is death, Finney rejects the claim that this death means physical death. "That this argument must assume, that there must be sin wherever there is suffering and death. But this assumption proves too much, as it would prove that mere animals have a sinful nature, or have committed actual sin. An argument that proves too much proves nothing."[33] He also rejects the idea that it is spiritual death where he takes this to mean the soul dies. Instead, he understands it to mean that the consequence of sin is sin itself, which is misery and the failure to achieve the highest happiness.

It is on the basis of this view of the free will that Finney developed his new methods for evangelism. Although these initially seemed to have results, the mid- to long-term results were much like those of the mega-preachers in the twentieth century. Most persons initially made a choice for Christianity and then fell away. It is in part due to this that continued revivals were necessary and created what came to be called the burned-over district in New York.

Finney linked his teaching to a political and legal philosophy. He said,

> The stability of our republican institutions must depend upon the progress of general intelligence and virtue. If in these respects the nation falls, if general intelligence, public and private virtue, sink to that point below which self-control becomes practicably impossible, we must fall back into monarchy, limited or absolute; or into civil or military despotism; just according to the national standard of intelligence and virtue. This is just as certain as that God governs the world, or that causes produce their effects.[34]

Yet there is disagreement on exactly what this virtue means and to what this general intelligence amounts. On Finney's view, the virtue is one aimed at happiness, and the definition of God he teaches is one that creates for his own happiness and happiness in general, is unable to bring about salvation apart from human cooperation, and has as the final goal for humans life in heaven. The idea that the goal in this life is to do what makes one happy is behind many of the social changes the country is currently seeing. The outward form of a republic could be retained while the content of the law is changed beyond recognition.

Finney's belief is that governments are not needed only because of sin. "If all men were perfectly holy and disposed to do right, the necessity for human governments would not be set aside, because this necessity is founded in the ignorance of mankind, though greatly aggravated by their wickedness."[35] Instead, governments are needed for securing the highest end. All such governments are either physical or moral. "All government is, and must be, either moral or physical; that is, all guidance and control must be exercised in accordance with either moral or physical law; for there can be no laws that are neither moral nor physical."[36] They are needed for securing the highest end and are therefore part of God's providential rule.[37]

Returning to his thoughts on reason, Finney states that it was given to humans to direct them to the highest end of life. "It gives him the idea of the eternal and the infinite."[38] Reason is used to make choices: "It consists in choosing self-gratification as an end, or for its own sake, instead of choosing, in accordance with the law of the reason and of God, the highest well-being of God and of the universe as an ultimate end."[39] In this description, Finney makes room for culpable ignorance. No one chooses misery when it is known to them to be misery.

> It cannot consist in malevolence, or in the choice of evil or misery as an ultimate end. This will appear, if we consider, that the choice of an end implies the choice of it, not for no reason, but for a reason, and for its own intrinsic value, or because the mind prizes it on its own account. But moral agents are so constituted, that they cannot regard misery as intrinsically valuable. They cannot, therefore, choose it as an ultimate end, nor prize it on its own account.[40]

Instead, all persons choose what they believe will make them happy. The true way of knowing this path to happiness is the moral law, which is the natural law. "That the moral law, as we have seen, is nothing else than the law of nature, or that rule of action which is founded, not in the will of God, but in the nature and relations of moral agents."[41] This is a rejection of divine command theory that grounds the law in the will of God. Instead, the law is grounded in the nature of things. God created things with their nature and, therefore, created the law. All of this was done for benevolence. Some critics pointed out that his theory of the law seems to remove God from the center. This need not be so in that he recognizes God as the creator of the nature of things. Instead, he has connected what is good to the nature of a being and, through that, to God the creator rather than directly to the will of God apart from the nature of things.

Part of human nature is rationality and choice. All men have the ideas of right and wrong and have words by which these ideas are expressed, and, perhaps, no idea among men more frequently reveals itself in words than that of oughtness or obligation.[42] This idea of obligation is universal and is manifest in the universal language of men.[43] It is an idea of pure reason, a simple concept that does not admit of definition. It is, to use a more recent term, *sui generis*.

The moral government that operates through these obligations and oughtness is the higher form of government, which is that one that will bring about the highest end. "We have just seen that the highest well-being of the universe demands, and is the end of moral government."[44] This moral government is best promoted through revivals. Indeed, until the final victory of good over evil, the millennial period, "The state of the world is still such, and probably will be till the millennium is fully come, that religion must be mainly promoted by means of revivals."[45] To achieve this millennium "depends on having a different sort of ministers, who are more thoroughly educated for their work."[46] Like Princeton, which had been founded to teach reformed orthodoxy and piety, Finney understood that an educational institution would be necessary to teach the theology he had developed.

Finney was confident that if his evangelical methods were used to start revivals, "If the whole Church, as a body, had gone to work ten years ago, and continued it as a few individuals, whom I could name, have done, there might not now have been an impenitent sinner in the land. The millennium would have fully come into the United States before this day."[47] It was possible, according to Finney, for good to overcome evil within the history of the United States and even before or during his day. This was undoubtedly due to the freedom of preaching that the United States offered in contrast to other lands. This revival work would spread to fill the whole world and bring about the millennium.

Finney has been identified as a postmillennialist, and in the eyes of competing theologians, this has given a negative stigma to postmillennialism. Michael Horton says, "The postmillennialism, Romanticism, idealism, and Pelagianism of the New Haven tradition fit perfectly with Social Darwinism's Hegelian eschatology. Departures from orthodoxy could be justified by the dogma of progress, since everyone embraced it."[48] Horton identifies progressive theology as beginning with Finney and taking a conservative and liberal branch: "Could it not be the case that the Pelagianism that combined with postmillennialism created the Social Gospel, while the merging of Finney and pre-millennialism led to Dispensational Fundamentalism."[49]

In general, this view simply says that good overcomes evil, that the knowledge of God fills the earth, and then Christ returns. Finney's own version is intricately related to his theory of the human will, God's purpose, the good as happiness, and the methods of evangelism. Although these forms might be rejected, it does not follow that postmillennialism is false or needs to be rejected.

We have studied Finney because he is considered by many scholars to be the most important American theologian in terms of formative influence. More importantly, we have studied him because he follows the formative outline of the Declaration of Independence in beginning with what he takes to be self-evident truths. From these, he proceeds to natural theology and the articulation of a moral law. His theory of salvation is central to his evangelical work, but he also drew out a theory of government in his systematic theology. Government aims at establishing the highest moral end: happiness or universal benevolence. Although he argued that ultimately it is the moral government that brings this to pass, we will see that many after him believed that the civil government could contribute greatly to bringing about the greatest happiness for humans. There are obvious connections between this idea of the human good as happiness and the use of law in the secular government in the name of creating a society in which people are able to pursue happiness. The social changes we see today are nested in terms of "progress" and "advancement" that are traceable to this approach to the human good. We turn next to liberal theology and its own views about what is self-evident, God, and the human good.

7 LIBERAL THEOLOGY AND LEGAL TRANSFORMATIONS

In order to preserve the distinction between personal belief and the function of the state, the Supreme Court, in *United States v. Ballard* (1944) distinguished between the truth of a religious claim and a person's believing that the religious claim is true. The Court said:

> Whether that is true or not is not the concern of this court and is not the concern of the jury – and they are going to be told so in their instructions. As far as this court sees the issue, it is immaterial what these defendants preached or wrote or taught in their classes. They are not going to be permitted to speculate on the actuality of the happening of those incidents. Now, I think I have made that as clear as I can. Therefore, the religious beliefs of these defendants cannot be an issue in this court.[1]

Instead, what the Court was focused on was whether a person believed the truth of their professed religious claims. "The issue is: did these defendants honestly and in good faith believe those things? If they did, they should be acquitted. I cannot make it any clearer than that."[2] It is only if the defendants did not believe what they professed that they could have committed the mail fraud of which they were accused.

> If these defendants did not believe those things, they did not believe that Jesus came down and dictated, or that Saint Germaine came down and dictated, did not believe the things that they wrote, the things that they preached, but used the mail for the purpose of getting money, the jury should find them guilty. Therefore, gentlemen, religion cannot come into this case.[3]

The alternative that the Court wanted to avoid was that of "heresy trials," in which persons are found guilty for believing what other people think is false. Instead, it maintained the right to form beliefs about life, death, and the afterlife that seemed best to the individual apart from what others thought. Furthermore, this included the right to believe things that cannot be proven by the individual. So there is both the right to believe and the right to believe what the person cannot prove. One reason for this is that the Court linked such beliefs to religious experiences, which are individual and particular and, therefore, cannot be judged by others:

> It embraces the right to maintain theories of life and of death and of the hereafter which are rank heresy to followers of the orthodox faiths. Heresy trials are foreign to our constitution. Men may believe what they cannot prove. They may not be put to the proof of their religious doctrines or beliefs. Religious experiences which are as real as life to some may be incomprehensible to others. Yet the fact that they may be beyond the ken of mortals does not mean that they can be made suspect before the law. Many take their gospel from the New Testament. But it would hardly be supposed that they could be tried before a jury charged with the duty of determining whether those teachings contained false representations. The miracles of the new testament, the divinity of Christ, life after death, the power of prayer are deep in the religious convictions of many.[4]

Interestingly, the limits of pursuing the truth of religious belief by the state are not simply due to the limitation of the authority and function of the state. Instead, they are rooted in the belief that there are no religious beliefs on which all people will agree. This could be understood either as a claim about whether knowledge on these matters is possible or about whether humans desire to know.

> If one could be sent to jail because a jury in a hostile environment found those teachings false, little indeed would be left of religious freedom. The fathers of the Constitution were not unaware of the varied and extreme views of religious sects, of the violence of disagreement among them, and of the lack of any one religious creed on which all men would agree. They fashioned a charter of government which envisaged the widest possible toleration of conflicting

> views. Man's relation to his god was made no concern of the state. He was granted the right to worship as he pleased and to answer to no man for the verity of his religious views. The religious views espoused by respondents might seem incredible, if not preposterous, to most people. But if those doctrines are subject to trial before a jury charged with finding their truth or falsity, then the same can be done with the religious beliefs of any sect.[5]

Once again, we see that the limits of government are based on the belief that agreement about religious belief is not possible and that there will always be divisions that must be balanced against each other. This gives a unique role to the lawyer both in society and in administering the state. Louis Brandeis said that the lawyer has one of the most useful roles in American society:

> But the legal profession does afford in America unusual opportunity for usefulness. That this has been so in the past, no one acquainted with the history of our institutions can for a moment doubt. The great achievement of the English-speaking people is the attainment of liberty through law. It is natural, therefore, that those who have been trained in the law should have borne an important part in that struggle for liberty and in the government which resulted. Accordingly, we find that in America the lawyer was in the earliest period almost omnipresent in the State. Nearly every great lawyer was then a statesman; and nearly every statesman, great or small, was a lawyer.[6]

He believed that it is through lawyers that progress will be made in society. "Nothing can better fit you for taking part in the solution of these problems, than the study and preeminently the practice of law. Those of you who feel drawn to that profession may rest assured that you will find in it an opportunity for usefulness which is probably unequalled."[7] Here, progress means material well-being and cannot mean the knowledge of the good, because the underlying skepticism about knowledge keeps that from being possible. The lawyer aids in progress through protecting freedom but also by shaping society. The curious tension is that in order to know how to be useful, one must know what is good for society, and this means that the good is knowable.

The Supreme Court's avoidance of heresy trials extends from wording by Thomas Jefferson. As we have already seen, the idea of pitting sect against sect as a means to protect freedom was there from the beginning. He said:

> Difference of opinion is advantageous in religion. The several sects form a *censor morum* over each other. Is uniformity attainable? Millions of innocent men, women, and children, since the introduction of Christianity, have been burnt, tortured, fined, imprisoned; yet we have not advanced one inch toward uniformity. What have been the effects of coercion? To make one half of the world fools, and the other half hypocrites. To support roguery and terror all over the earth. Let us reflect that it is inhabited by a thousand millions of people. That these profess probably a thousand different systems of religion. That ours is but one of that thousand.[8]

This dichotomy between either heresy trials on the one hand or skepticism on the other is a false dichotomy that does not help in identifying what beliefs are necessarily presupposed by government and law. It does not help in dealing with the problem of what can be known. Instead, both sides of the dichotomy are based on skepticism. Of course, coercion is never of any use because it is an informal fallacy: appeal to fear. Professing a statement to be true out of fear of consequences does not make it true.

In this chapter, we are going to look at the theologian Paul Tillich. The Supreme Court relied on Tillich's definition of religion in the case *United States v. Seeger*. Tillich defines religion in a way that gets to what is common among all religions. Instead of defining religion in terms of "God" he defines it in terms of "ultimate concern" which gets closer to what is universal. He seeks to articulate a common ground that goes beyond any specific religious creed. In order to do this, he tries to identify what he believes are the significant challenges of his day.

PAUL TILLICH

Paul Tillich begins his systematic theology by taking stock of where he sees the current state of theology and the problems that arise in that context. He views fundamentalism, a combination of older orthodoxy and piety, as a system holding to the past with no relevant application to the present. He sees empirical theology as having taken over the search for objectivity but still needing to explain its relevance. Contemporary theology must resolve the tension between holding to eternal truths and applying these to a particular context in history. He proposes a solution to these deadlocks in theology and to this tension between truth and application.

One of the tensions that Tillich faces is between building on what has come before in historic Christianity and compromising through reinterpretation in order to meet the attitudes of the day. "Theology, as a function of the Christian church, must serve the needs of the church. A theological system is supposed to satisfy two basic needs: the statement of the truth of the Christian message and the interpretation of this truth for every new generation."[9] There is every reason to apply the insights of historic Christianity to the challenges of each period. However, in order to do this, one must build consistently on what has come before, and we will see instead that Tillich gives a very new vision of Christianity that fits better with the term *pantheism* than with *theism.*

Tillich recognizes the need both for common ground and how a mistaken identification of common ground leads to problem. There has always been a fear that accepting common ground somehow diminishes the need for regeneration and the teaching that all are dead in their trespasses and sins. The teaching of the American great awakenings was that a religious experience of regeneration was necessary. This experience cannot itself be common ground, because it is particular and not shared by all. Tillich phrases it this way:

> Apologetics presupposes common ground, however vague it may be. But kerygmatic theologians are inclined to deny any common ground with those outside the "theological circle." They are afraid that the common ground will destroy the uniqueness of the message. They point to the early Christian Apologists who saw a common ground in the acceptance of the Logos; they point to the Alexandrian school which found a common ground in Platonism; they point to Thomas Aquinas' use of Aristotle; above all, they point to the common ground which apologetic theology believed itself to have found with the philosophy of the Enlightenment, with Romanticism, with Hegelianism and Kantianism, with humanism and naturalism.[10]

He sees the attempt to find common ground between theology and the scientific method as a failure.

> Attempts to elaborate a theology as an empirical-inductive or a metaphysical deductive "science," or as a combination of both, have given ample evidence that no such an attempt can succeed. In every assumedly scientific theology there is a point where individual experience, traditional valuation, and personal commitment must decide the issue.[11]

Instead, he argues that there is a mystical or intuitional beginning point for any theology and that this creates a theological circle that cannot be avoided.

> In both the empirical and the metaphysical approaches, as well as in the much more numerous cases of their mixture, it can be observed that the a priori which directs the induction and the deduction is a type of mystical experience ... The theological concepts of both idealists and naturalists are rooted in a "mystical a priori," an awareness of something that transcends the cleavage between subject and object ... This is the circle which no religious philosopher can escape. And it is by no means a vicious one. Every understanding of spiritual things is circular.[12]

In one way, this is simply a description of how systems work. The doctrine of the theological circle is a system, it is logically connected, so that each part presupposes the others.[13] Yet the image of a circle denies that some beliefs are more basic than others. Some beliefs are presupposed by the rest of the system, and those that are presupposed by the entire system but do not themselves have further presuppositions are the most basic. For Tillich, this still ends in a circle, because he believes that one accepts these most basic beliefs through a mystical or intuitive move and not for any other reason. In this sense, there can be no rational justification for one set of basic beliefs over another, nor can one communicate what is entirely personal in this mystical acceptance. In taking this as his beginning point, he is setting aside reason and the cognitive in favor of what is noncognitive. We can see this in his definition of religion.

> Ultimate concern is the abstract translation of the great commandment: "The Lord, our God, the Lord is one; and you shall love the

> Lord your God with all your heart, and with all your soul and with all your mind, and with all your strength." The religious concern is ultimate; it excludes all other concerns from ultimate significance; it makes them preliminary. The ultimate concern is unconditional, independent of any conditions of character, desire, or circumstance. The unconditional concern is total: no part of ourselves or of our world is excluded from it; there is no "place" to flee from it. The total concern is infinite: no moment of relaxation and rest is possible in the face of a religious concern which is ultimate, unconditional, total, and infinite.[14]

To make "concern" the starting point is to begin with the noncognitive. He says,

> The word "concern" points to the "existential" character of religious experience ... That which is ultimate gives itself only to the attitude of ultimate concern ... It is the object of total surrender, demanding also the surrender of our subjectivity while we look at it. It is a matter of infinite passion and interest (Kierkegaard), making us its object whenever we try to make it our object ... Of course, in every concern there is *something* about which one is concerned; but this something should not appear as a separated object which could be known and handled without concern.[15]

When theology does advance to make propositions, they are grounded in this noncognitive beginning of ultimate concern. "This, then, is the first formal criterion of theology: *The object of theology is what concerns us ultimately. Only those propositions are theological which deal with their object in so far as it can become a matter of ultimate concern for us.*"[16] He helps us better understand this ultimate concern by identifying it with that which deals with being or non-being for us.[17] This goes beyond God as a particular being and to that which transcends being itself.

Even with this noncognitive start and the affirmation of a circle rather than a presupposition system, Tillich does turn to thinking as one feature of common ground between humans. He particularly takes up the term *logos* as the *reasoning* about God. He explicitly rejects the placement of religion into the emotional or nonrational areas of life as an attempt to avoid conflict between science and religion:

> If taken in the broadest sense of the word, theology, the *logos* or the reasoning about *theos* (God and divine things), is as old as religion.

> Thinking pervades all the spiritual activities of man. Man would not be spiritual without words, thoughts, concepts. This is especially true in religion, the all-embracing function of man's spiritual life ... The banishment of religion into the nonrational corner of subjective emotions in order to have the realms of thought and action free from religious interference was an easy way of escaping the conflicts between religious tradition and modern thought. But this was a death sentence against religion, and religion did not and could not accept it.[18]

Tillich claims that Christian theology is *the* theology because its message resolves the tension between the absolutely concrete and the absolutely universal.[19] "The basis of this claim is the Christian doctrine that the Logos became flesh, that the principle of the divine self-revelation has become manifest in the event 'Jesus as the Christ.' If this message is true, Christian theology has received a foundation which transcends the foundation of any other theology and which itself cannot be transcended."[20] Tillich believes the *logos* is absolutely universal but that Jesus Christ makes it absolutely concrete. "But it is necessary to accept the vision of early Christianity that if Jesus is called the Christ he must represent everything particular and must be the point of identity between the absolutely concrete and the absolutely universal."[21]

In this organization of Christian thinking, there is a break with historic Christianity's teaching about the need for Christ. We do not see in Tillich anything about vicarious atonement or the covenant between God and man. Nor is there mention of the idea that humans are inexcusable before God and in need of redemption rather than in need of more information from God. The Christ event is a manifestation of God to humans, who could not know about the entirely universal without this concrete example. As such, Tillich's theology is not an application of historic Christianity to contemporary issues but is a reformulation of Christian terms and application of them to challenges from sources such as existentialism.

In our examination of Thomas Reid, we saw that he raised the question of what must be presupposed for intelligibility. Tillich also asks this question:

> The suggestion here is to call philosophy *that cognitive approach to reality in which reality as such is the object*. Reality as such, or reality

> as a whole, is not the whole of reality; it is the structure which makes reality a whole and therefore a potential object of knowledge. Inquiring into the nature of reality as such means inquiring into those structures, categories, and concepts which are presupposed in the cognitive encounter with every realm of reality. From this point of view philosophy is by definition critical ... The question regarding the character of the general structures that make experience possible is always the same. It is *the* philosophical question.[22]

He calls this *the* philosophical question, and he borrows his answer from Kant, who spoke about the need to presuppose categories such as space and time in order to make experience intelligible. However, prior to these categories is the ability to form concepts about categories. This is the use of reason. Reason is presupposed in any meaningful statement because it is by reason that we form concepts (distinguish between *a* and *non-a*) and put these together into judgments and arguments. Tillich identifies *logos* with the reasoning about God. He says: "Therefore, this *logos* is common; every reasonable being participates in it, uses it in asking questions and criticizing the answers received."[23]

At one moment, he rejects the possibility of a conflict between philosophy and theology because they share no common ground over which to conflict. But then he also affirms that the same logos that is studied by the one is also taught by the other:

> A conflict presupposes a common basis on which to fight. But there is no common basis between theology and philosophy ... Thus there is no conflict between theology and philosophy, and there is no synthesis either – for exactly the same reason which insures that there will be no conflict. A common basis is lacking. The idea of a synthesis between theology and philosophy has led to the dream of a "Christian philosophy." The term is ambiguous ... Therefore, the idea of a "Christian philosophy" in the narrower sense of a philosophy which is intentionally Christian must be rejected ... Christianity does not need a "Christian philosophy" in the narrower sense of the word. The Christian claim that the *logos* who has become concrete in Jesus as the Christ is at the same time the universal *logos* includes the claim that wherever the *logos* is at work it agrees with the Christian message. No philosophy which is obedient to the universal *logos* can contradict the concrete *logos*, the Logos "who became flesh."[24]

When we look at John 1, we see that the *logos* is described as the eternal Word of God that was with God in the beginning and through whom all things were made; this *logos* is made known in the creation; this *logos* is given in scripture; and because these were rejected, the *logos* becomes incarnate. Tillich has good reason to start with the *logos*, but his analysis of it does not address the inexcusability of humans in rejecting the *logos* that makes God known as reason, general revelation, and then redemptive revelation and Christ. This is more than the usual identification of the *logos* with either the Bible or Christ alone. There is a sense in which Tillich wants to suggest a fuller account of the logos when he says: "If the 'Word of God' or the 'act of revelation' is called the source of systematic theology, it must be emphasized that the 'Word of God' is not limited to the words of a book and that that act of revelation is not the 'inspiring' of a 'book of revelations,' even if the book is the document of the final 'Word of God.'"[25]

Even so, what Tillich comes to mean is the sense of intuition mentioned earlier. The individual has an encounter with reality that is shaped by his educational and cultural setting.[26] It is in this encounter that the logos operates above and beyond the text of the Bible. Tillich develops what he calls the method of correlation:

> In using the method of correlation, systematic theology proceeds in the following way: it makes an analysis of the human situation out of which the existential questions arise, and it demonstrates that the symbols used in the Christian message are the answers to these questions. The analysis of the human situation is done in terms which today are called "existential." Such analyses are much older than existentialism; they are, indeed, as old as man's thinking about himself, and they have been expressed in various kinds of conceptualization since the beginning of philosophy ... The theologian organizes these materials in relation to the answer given by the Christian message. In the light of this message he may make an analysis of existence which is more penetrating than that of most philosophers. Nevertheless, it remains a philosophical analysis.[27]

The issue is whether the theologian has correctly understood the Christian message. Tillich's form seems to be a kind of mix between Kant and Heidegger. Christian revelation is given because humans cannot know by reason. Reason, according to Tillich, is finite and fallible.

> But reason is not merely finite. It is true that reason, along with all things and events, is subject to the conditions of existence. It contradicts itself and is threatened with disruption and self-destruction. Its elements move against each other. But this is only one side of the picture. In the actual life of reason its basic structure is never completely lost. If it were lost, mind as well as reality would have been destroyed in the very moment of their coming into existence. In the actual life of reason essential and existential forces, forces of creation and forces of destruction, are united and disunited at the same time. These conflicts in actual reason supply the content for a justifiable theological criticism of reason … it should, at the same time, force reason to acknowledge its own existential predicament out of which the quest for revelation arises.[28]

It is because of this that revelation is needed. "The catastrophe of autonomous reason is complete. Neither autonomy nor heteronomy, isolated and in conflict, can give the answer."[29] Revelation is necessary to have knowledge of God. "Revelation is the manifestation of the ground of being for human knowledge… Knowing is a form of union. In every act of knowledge the knower and that which is known are united; the gap between subject and object is overcome. The subject 'grasps' the object, adapts it to itself, and at the same time, adapts itself to the object."[30]

Christ becomes a kind of metaphor that reveals to us our condition before God. Christ is the logos but in the sense that all things are divine.

> Knowledge is more than fulfilling; it also transforms and heals … It is at least probable that Socrates knew what every schoolboy knows – that some people act against their better knowledge … He who knows God or the Christ in the sense of being grasped by him and being united with him does the good. He who knows the essential structure of things in the sense of having received their meaning and power acts according to them; he does the good, even if he has to die for it.[31]

In this analysis there is no room for the inexcusability of unbelief and, therefore, no need for the atoning work of Christ. Instead, knowledge as revelation is a kind of intuition that unites humans to God. "Knowledge stands in a dilemma; controlling knowledge is safe but not ultimately significant, while receiving knowledge can be ultimately significant, but it cannot give certainty … revelation claims to give truth which is both certain and of ultimate concern."[32]

Tillich denies that reason applies to being, that reason is ontological. There is nothing, according to him, that is self-evident and applies to the concrete. He says:

> The verification of principles of ontological reason has the character neither of rational self-evidence nor of a pragmatic test. Rational self-evidence cannot be attributed to a principle which contains more than the mere form of rationality, as, for instance, Kant's categorical imperative. Every concrete principle, every category and norm, which expresses more than pure rationality is subject to experimental or experiential verification. It is not self-evident, even if it contains a self-evident element (which, however, cannot be abstracted from it).[33]

He also denies that there is a natural revelation. Natural revelation is a contradiction in terms, he says. If it is natural, then it is not revelation, because revelation involves the ecstatic and miraculous. What can be known by natural knowledge of the self and of the world cannot lead to knowledge of the ground of being or the highest good.

> It can lead to the question of the ground of being, and that is what so-called natural theology can do and must do. But this question is asked neither by natural revelation nor by natural theology. It is the question of reason about its own ground and abyss. It is asked by reason, but reason cannot answer it. Revelation can answer it. And this answer is based neither on a so-called natural revelation nor on a so-called natural theology.[34]

It is in these quotes that we can see Tillich relying on intuition and the religious experience and at the same time denying that there is anything self-evident (about God or the good) or that reason can be used to know God or the good. Instead, revelation is needed for these. This might sound similar to some forms of theistic fideism. However, we will see that Tillich takes a pantheistic turn in identifying all things with God.

He does not do this in a straightforward way. He wants to avoid speaking about God as a being because he believes this makes God just one more object in the universe. In phrasing things this way, he borrows the idea of *being* from Heidegger. The latter speaks about *being* in one specific way: finite, temporal, changeable being. And so it would be correct to affirm that God cannot be a *being* in this sense since God is not finite, temporal, or changeable. "Theologians make God an object by asking if God exists."[35] Therefore, Tillich speaks of God as the ground of being. It might be easier to use the historical means of speaking about the being of God as infinite, eternal, and unchangeable so as to distinguish God from created being. Since Tillich does not do this, he is not able to speak of *kind of being* in this sense but instead only either of finite, temporal, and changeable being or the ground of this being. This leads him and others who take this line to end up in pantheism, where finite being is somehow part of God or an emanation of God or contains the divine. The claim is also that reason is limited to finite, temporal, and changeable being and, therefore, cannot know God:

> The categories of experience are categories of finitude. They do not enable human reason to grasp reality-in-itself; but they do enable man to grasp his world, the totality of the phenomena which appear to him and which constitute his actual experience. The main category of finitude is time. Being finite means being temporal. Reason cannot break through the limits of temporality and reach the eternal, just as it cannot break through the limits of causality, space, substance, in order to teach the first cause, absolute space, universal substance.[36]

Tillich notes this in identifying God as eternal and then asking what it means for humans to have eternal life:

> God is eternal; this is the decisive characteristic of those qualities which make him God. He is subjected neither to the temporal process nor with it to the structure of finitude... This leads immediately to the question: How is the eternal God, who is also the living God, related to Eternal Life, which is the inner aim of all creatures? There cannot be two eternal life processes parallel to each other, and the New Testament excludes this idea by calling God alone the "eternal one." The only possible answer is that Eternal Life is life in the eternal, life in God.[37]

Creation itself is eternal, without beginning, and is an act of love. "The eternal act of creation is driven by a love which finds fulfillment only through the other one who has the freedom to reject and accept love. God, so to speak, drives toward the actualization and essentialization of everything that has being."[38] This is the Christian message, according to Tillich. It has no consistent relation to historic Christianity. Tillich might argue that it is Christianity applied to current challenges, but that can be done in a way that is consistent with historic Christianity. Instead, this view of Christianity follows from Tillich's metaphysics, which follows from his epistemology. "The marks of revelation – mystery, miracle, and ecstasy – are present in every true prayer. Speaking to God and receiving an answer is an ecstatic and miraculous experience; it transcends all ordinary structures of subjective and objective reason. It is the presence of the mystery of being and an actualization of our ultimate concern."[39]

The problem is that if we cannot know our ultimate concern except through this intuition or experience, then we cannot be held responsible for failing to know it, because not all persons have this intuition, and this intuition can be interpreted in many different ways. "Revelation is the manifestation of the mystery of being for the cognitive function of human reason … Since the knowledge of revelation cannot be separated from the situation of revelation, it cannot be introduced into the context of ordinary knowledge as an addition."[40]

Tillich is offering one interpretation of this intuition. But is it a coherent interpretation? It is one more form of monism that claims all being is ultimately one and all being is eternal. In order to justify this claim, he must also limit human reason, because reason finds contradictions in this form of monism.

> Reason, philosophy as stating the question, theology and revelation as giving answers, ultimate concern, absolute faith, God as ground of being but beyond being, theological theism does not answer the concern of anxiety about being and non-being but God beyond being does, God beyond subject-object distinction by preceding it, considered by some a pantheist or even an atheist. Dialectic reading of history, conservative, fundamentalist, being and non-being, category mistakes about ontology and epistemology and being and non-being and participating in.[41]

Philosophy, as the critical use of reason to test a belief for meaning, cannot offer any help, because according to Tillich, it leads to contradictory questions. It leads to an infinite regress of questions about where being has come from:

> Philosophy asks the question of being as being. It investigates the character of everything that is in so far as it is. This is its basic task, and the answer it provides determines the analysis of all special forms of being. It is "first philosophy," ... "Why is there something; why not nothing?" But in this form the question is meaningless, for every possible answer would be subject to the same question in an infinite regression. Thought must start with being; it cannot go behind it, as the form of the question itself shows. If one asks why there *is* not nothing, one attributes being even to nothing.[42]

Asking "where did that come from?" is a natural question even asked by children. But it leads to an infinite regress of answers. Even if it led to God, "it cannot be stopped even by a god who is supposed to be the answer to the entire series. For this god must ask himself, 'Where have I come from? (Kant). Even a highest being must ask the question of its own cause, indicating thereby its partial nonbeing."[43]

This confuses temporal being with eternal being. If a being is eternal, had no beginning, then it is the highest being, and it need not ask the question "where have I come from?" This failure to distinguish temporal and eternal being leads to Tillich's problem in limiting reason and in seeking to go being beyond to the ground of being. Reason shows that only some is eternal, God, while all else is created and temporal. This does not lead to an infinite regress of questions because eternal being stops that question.

Tillich also relies on his epistemology and metaphysics to give an ethical theory. He says:

> This distinction between natural and revealed law is ethically irrelevant, because according to classical Protestant theology, the Ten Commandments, as well as the commandments of the Sermon on the Mount, are restatements of the natural law, the "law of love," after periods in which it was partly forgotten, partly distorted. Their substance is the natural law, or in our terminology, man's essential nature standing against him in his existential estrangement. If formulated in commandments, this law never reaches the here and

> now of a particular decision. With respect to it, the commandment may be right in a special situation just because of its prohibitive form. Every moral decision demands a partial liberation from the stated moral law. Every moral decision is a risk because there is no guarantee that it fulfills the law of love, the unconditional demand coming from the encounter with the other. This risk must be taken, but if it is taken the question arises, how is it possible to teach personal self-integration under these circumstances? There is no answer to this question within the realm of man's moral life and its ambiguities.[44]

As in all instances of appealing to "love," this term must be defined. The "law of love" is defined in the New Testament as keeping the commandments of God. "If you love me you will keep my commandments."[45] To love someone is to seek what is good for them. Therefore, in order to love, one must know what is good. However, Tillich gives us his description of the human condition: "It is accepted as the expression of what man essentially or by creation is. It is transcended in its form as law, that is, as that which stands against man in his existential estrangement, as commandment and threat."[46]

This existential estrangement is resolved, in Tillich's view, through the intuition or experience of the ground of being as the ultimate concern. It is resolved in finding one's unity in God's eternal life. The law, the moral law and its civil application, becomes a circumstance wherein man's self-integration is the goal. The law must be applied in a way that affirms the need for this self-integration, and this can appear to lead to contradictions in the law. Tillich believes speaking of the "law of love" overcomes these problems. However, self-integration is itself a desire for integrity. Integrity is a concern for consistency – in this case, consistency with one's self. To be consistent in this way requires knowing the nature of the self, knowing that the self is created by God. Integrity is a requirement of reason. If Tillich has on the one hand abandoned reason, then he cannot consistently require integrity at another point. He has introduced into the idea of the moral law the focus on human self-integration that comes to be understood as self-expression. No longer is the moral law the guide to the highest good, but instead, the expression of the self as part of the divine is thought to be good. Although Tillich speaks of redemption, this redemption is not from a state of not seeking, not understanding, and not doing what is right but from a state of not identifying as divine to a state of doing so. As such, self-expression can mean almost anything. It cannot consistently be limited, because humans are identified with God. Unlike historic Christianity, Tillich does not believe that humans are inexcusable before God for unbelief and violating the moral law. Instead, self-expression cannot be limited by what are supposedly mere constructs from the past, and we can see how this is being applied in current social and legal changes.

And so we see that a leading American theologian in the twentieth century has proposed a theology that denies that it is self-evident that God created humans. It rests on an epistemology of intuition that limits reason and rejects natural theology. Humans cannot know the highest good except through revelation, which is a kind of experience. This is a theologian that the Supreme Court relied upon to define religion. It seems that his beliefs about self-expression continue to be influential.

That Tillich was influential does not mean that other, more historic forms of Christianity did not persist in the twentieth century. But it does show that the reliance on intuition we saw in Emerson and Darwin continued in the twentieth century. I am tracing this strand of thinking since it has become influential both in society and in legal decisions. There continue to be disagreements about the nature of God and the highest good. Greater disunity, rather than greater unity, seems to be the direction of things. This is true even though the claim is that more self-expression is available and is good. In the next chapter, we will look at an attempt to find resolution by synthesizing the claims of competing religions.

8 SECULAR AND RELIGIOUS GOODS IN THE TWENTIETH CENTURY

Perhaps the best-known and most contentious Supreme Court decision remains the *Roe v. Wade* decision of 1973. Although this decision can be said to be secular, it involved important religious considerations. Specifically, the majority decision spent time considering various beliefs about the definition of a human, human soul, and person. The idea that the soul was added to the unborn child some time after conception was called "quickening."

> The common law. It is undisputed that at common law, abortion performed before "quickening" – the first recognizable movement of the fetus in utero, appearing usually from the 16th to the 18th week of pregnancy – was not an indictable offense. The absence of a common-law crime for pre-quickening abortion appears to have developed from a confluence of earlier philosophical, theological, and civil and canon law concepts of when life begins. These disciplines variously approached the question in terms of the point at which the embryo or fetus became "formed" or recognizably human, or in terms of when a "person" came into being, that is, infused with a "soul" or "animated." A loose consensus evolved in early English law that these events occurred at some point between conception and live birth. This was "mediate animation." Although Christian theology and the canon law came to fix the point of animation at 40 days for a male and 80 days for a female, a view that persisted until the 19th century, there was otherwise little agreement about the precise time of formation or animation. There was agreement, however, that prior to this point the fetus was to be regarded as part of the mother, and its destruction, therefore, was

> not homicide. Due to continued uncertainty about the precise time when animation occurred, to the lack of any empirical basis for the 40-80-day view, and perhaps to Aquinas' definition of movement as one of the two first principles of life, Bracton focused upon quickening as the critical point. The significance of quickening was echoed by later common-law scholars and found its way into the received common law in this country.[1]

Arguing from these conflicting beliefs, the Court reached a position of skepticism about the human soul and person. "We need not resolve the difficult question of when life begins. When those trained in the respective disciplines of medicine, philosophy, and theology are unable to arrive at any consensus, the judiciary, at this point in the development of man's knowledge, is not in a position to speculate as to the answer."[2] It is interesting that it noted both that there is no consensus and no knowledge. Of course, there could be consensus but not knowledge. And there can be knowledge even when there is no consensus. But the point of the Court was one of skepticism about the human soul and person.

> It is thus apparent that at common law, at the time of the adoption of our constitution, and throughout the major portion of the 19th century, abortion was viewed with less disfavor than under most American statutes currently in effect. Phrasing it another way, a woman enjoyed a substantially broader right to terminate a pregnancy than she does in most states today.[3]

The Court focused on the word "person" in the Fourteenth Amendment and decided that it did not apply to the unborn. "All this, together with our observation, supra, that throughout the major portion of the 19th century prevailing legal abortion practices were far freer than they are today, persuades us that the word 'person,' as used in the Fourteenth Amendment, does not include the unborn."[4] Deciding that the Fourteenth Amendment only applies to persons, and the unborn are not persons, led the Court to decide that there is a right to privacy in a mother's decision about keeping the baby. "This right of privacy, whether it be founded in the Fourteenth Amendment's concept of personal liberty and restrictions upon state action, as we feel it is, or, as the district court determined, in the Ninth Amendment's reservation of rights to the people, is broad enough to encompass a woman's decision whether or not to terminate her pregnancy."[5]

Additionally, the Court considered the undue suffering that would be imposed on a mother if her child's life were protected when she did not want to have the baby.

> The detriment that the state would impose upon the pregnant woman by denying this choice altogether is apparent. Specific and direct harm medically diagnosable even in early pregnancy may be involved. Maternity, or additional off-spring, may force upon the woman a distressful life and future. Psychological harm may be imminent. Mental and physical health may be taxed by child care. There is also the distress, for all concerned, associated with the unwanted child, and there is the problem of bringing a child into a family already unable, psychologically and otherwise, to care for it. In other cases, as in this one, the additional difficulties and continuing stigma factors the woman and her responsible physician necessarily will consider in consultation.[6]

Again, this position of skepticism about whether the baby is a person was justified by appealing to various competing views on the matter. A pragmatic solution was taken in focusing on the time of viability, when the baby could live outside of the mother.

> It should be sufficient to note briefly the wide divergence of thinking on this most sensitive and difficult question. There has always been strong support for the view that life does not begin until live birth. This was the belief of the Stoics. It appears to be the predominant, though not the unanimous, attitude of the Jewish faith. It may be taken to represent also the position of a large segment of the Protestant community, insofar as that can be ascertained; organized groups that have taken a formal position on the abortion issue have generally regarded abortion as a matter for the conscience of the individual and her family. As we have noted, the common law found greater significance in quickening. Physicians and their scientific colleagues have regarded that event with less interest and have tended to focus either upon conception, upon live birth, or upon the interim point at which the fetus becomes "viable," that is, potentially able to live outside the mother's womb, albeit with artificial aid. Viability is usually placed at about seven months (28 weeks) but may occur earlier, even at 24 weeks.[7]

Besides relying on the skepticism of competing views, the Court also dismissed the idea that life begins at conception because it was linked to the "ensoulment" theory that seems religious and not scientific. This view says that the being becomes a human when the soul is introduced.

> The latter is now, of course, the official belief of the Catholic Church. As one brief amicus discloses, this is a view strongly held by many non-Catholics as well, and by many physicians. Substantial problems for precise definition of this view are posed, however, by new embryological data that purport to indicate that conception is a 'process' over time, rather than an event, and by new medical techniques such as implantation of embryos, artificial insemination, and even artificial wombs.[8]

The Court quoted St. Augustine to justify its skepticism about when ensoulment, if there is such a thing, occurs: "The theological debate was reflected in the writings of St. Augustine, who made a distinction between embryo inanimatus, not yet endowed with a soul, and embryo animatus. He may have drawn upon Exodus 21:22. At one point, however, he expressed the view that human powers cannot determine the point during fetal development at which the critical change occurs."[9]

And so the conclusion with respect to the state's role in protecting the unborn child is: "With respect to the state's important and legitimate interest in potential life, the 'compelling' point is at viability. This is so because the fetus then presumably has the capability of meaningful life outside the mother's womb."[10]

The Court's decision does not require a mother to have an abortion and, therefore, it does not explain, in itself, the history of abortion in America since 1973. However, its reasoning process is illuminating. By taking a skeptical position, it did not exempt itself from taking a position by implication. If the unborn is a person at conception, then the reasoning of the Court would be that the child should be protected. However, the Court decided that it is not a person at that time. It justified this by arguing that there are many competing views, and so no one seems to know. Instead, it took a pragmatic solution in making viability the standard for protection by the state. Advancements since

1973 have changed when an unborn child is viable, making it an earlier period of the pregnancy than at that time.

FAITH AND POSTMODERNITY

As we have seen in this book, this kind of skepticism is not new to American legal reasoning about basic beliefs. However, just as in this case, this skepticism does end up taking a position on matters of basic beliefs. In this chapter, we are going to consider theologian John Cobb, who proposed a theology of synthesis that sought to show how what appear to be competing religions share basic beliefs.

This is an appropriate last theologian to consider because it will exhaust the kinds of solutions we can consider. From the beginning, sect was set against sect to insure that no majority would be able to gain authority and use it to coerce others in matters of belief. We have seen that attempts were made to rely on intuition and common sense in articulating basic beliefs used to support competing worldviews. In Tillich and Emerson, Christian terms were used but with new meaning. Another approach is to argue that Christianity as one religion among many is similar to other religions, all of which teach similar basic beliefs.

In the second half of the twentieth century, it became increasingly popular to speak of postmodernity. Just as the Founders had the devastation of the Wars of Religion in mind, so, too, the World Wars of the first half of the twentieth century left the sense that the modern world had failed. John Cobb puts it this way:

> Modernity, rather than being regarded as the norm for human society toward which all history has been aiming and into which all societies should be ushered – forcibly if necessary – is instead increasingly seen as an aberration. A new respect for the wisdom of traditional societies is growing as we realize that they have endured for thousands of years and that, by contrast, the existence of modern civilization for even another century seems doubtful. Likewise, modernism as a worldview is less and less seen as The Final Truth, in comparison with which all divergent worldviews are automatically regarded as "superstitious." The modern worldview

> is increasingly relativized to the status of one among many, useful for some purposes, inadequate for others.[11]

Interestingly, the postmodern world is one that shares the skepticism that we have seen as so important in American history:

> The reconstructive activity of this type of postmodern thought is not limited to a revised worldview. It is equally concerned with a postmodern world that will both support and be supported by the new worldview. A postmodern world will involve postmodern persons, with a postmodern spirituality, on the one hand, and a postmodern society, ultimately a postmodern global order, on the other. Going beyond the modern world will involve transcending its individualism, anthropocentrism, patriarchy, economism, consumerism, nationalism, and militarism. Reconstructive postmodern thought provides support for the ethnic, ecological, feminist, peace, and other emancipatory movements of our time, while stressing that the inclusive emancipation must be from the destructive features of modernity itself.[12]

Cobb is outlining a worldview deduced from his basic beliefs. The question is why should we accept these basic beliefs. He thinks that they are the implications of process theology, which teaches that all is one and all is change.

PROCESS THEOLOGY

Cobb relies on the process theology of Alfred North Whitehead to understand Christianity and its relation to other religions. Like what we saw in Emerson and Tillich, Whitehead's process theology is monistic and not theistic. Cobb sets Whitehead's theology against the secularization that continued in postmodernity:

> The dominant forms of postmodernism have continued the secularizing process of modernity. They have no place for a holy or divine reality. This neglect is reinforced by their rejection of realism in general and their avoidance of the cosmological project. Whitehead, on the other hand, reopened the discussion of God. He rejected the dominant understanding of God in both the classical and the modern worlds. In particular he opposed the idea of

> an omnipotent deity controlling everything and unaffected by what happens in the world. But he found a place for a pervasive divine indwelling in all things, calling them into a process of becoming, giving them freedom to transcend their past, and receiving them as they perish, moment by moment, into the divine life.[13]

One of the objections of postmodern thinkers to modernity is the idea that there is a true worldview. This is applied to all "totalizing" claims but especially to Christianity. Postmodern thinkers want to contextualize all knowledge claims into a specific historical and cultural setting and analyze them in terms of power relations. Something is said to be true insofar as it advances a particular power structure. John Cobb adopts this approach in his approach to Christianity:

> As modernity advanced, the claim that Christianity is superior to other religious traditions and communities lost its persuasiveness. That claim has been superseded by the view that all the great religious traditions are paths to the same goal. As paths they are quite different, but their success in reaching the goal is relatively equal. The goal may be understood as loving communion with neighbors, as proper response to the holy, as union with ultimate reality, or, more recently, as transformation from ego-centeredness to centeredness in the Real.[14]

In this approach, there are only so many traditions, and these cannot be analyzed for truth because the standards for truth are tradition relative. Cobb believes that one can be within the Christian tradition in the sense of being in the Christian community, which teaches an orientation to the ultimate in contrast to the self and the love of neighbor where this means helping others overcome natural evil.

> Since Christianity offers a successful and effective path to the ultimate goal, those who have been formed by the Christian tradition have every reason to continue to pursue that path. From a postmodern perspective, this effort to find or impose unity on diverse communities is objectionable. However generous the intention, the effect is hegemonic. Inevitably, the goal that is affirmed as common to all expresses the values of the writer and silences the voices of those who have other priorities and commitments. This is true even if some members of the diverse traditions can recognize their ends in what is asserted to be the universal goal.[15]

TRADITION AND COMMUNITY

In this sense, postmodernity is a return to tradition. There are just many different traditions that are incommensurable. When one tradition becomes a majority, it uses its power to influence others. However, its becoming a majority has nothing to do with its being true. Being a Christian is to accept the Christian tradition but does not require thinking Christianity is true while other religions are false:

> The influence of postmodernism on Christian theology is most visible among those who have renounced any universal claims. They recognize Christianity as one community among others, with its own distinctive traditions and practices. To be a Christian is not to compare Christianity with others and make claims either to superiority or to equality. It is not to try to impose Christian teachings on society as a whole. It is to immerse oneself in one's own community, appropriating its values and meanings more deeply, and living from its stories and rituals. The argument for this understanding of Christianity is familiar to many postmodernists. It begins with the rejection of the notion that language mirrors an objective and independent reality. According to this view, there is no access apart from language to a "real" world, and hence there can be no correspondence of language to that world. Instead, the world we inhabit is a linguistic one. This means that Christian doctrines are not to be viewed as assertions about how things are in and of themselves. They are not to be believed in this sense. Instead, they constitute a system of symbols and meanings that can order understanding and life. Christianity thus understands itself as a cultural-linguistic system.[16]

The idea that Christianity is a linguistic community is the idea that all ideas are relative to language and that language is not ontological, does not apply to being. Languages are historical constructs. From this is drawn the conclusion that because they are historical constructs, they are not true or false, or one of them is not true while others are false. However, it could be true that languages are developed historically but also that they are ways of expressing ideas or concepts and that these concepts are meant to apply to reality.

To say that faith is part of a community life is to say that faith is an activity or way of living and is not a matter of true or false beliefs.

Instead, faith is noncognitive. It is a kind of *knowing how* rather than a *knowing that*. It is like knowing how to bake bread. At each step, the baker knows how much flour to add, or salt, or what the crust should like look when it is done baking. However, the baker might not be able to explain this process.

It is true that there are many such ways of knowing how. Living out a faith is perhaps one of them. However, behind such activities remain the basic questions. Answers to these questions shape which faith one lives. In the analogy of the bread, they shape what kind of bread is being made. So while it is true that there are many ways of *knowing how* in life, this does not exclude the reality that we must still deal with knowing what is true in order to know if we are living out the correct faith. Different basic truths lead to different kinds of lived faiths.

Languages, linguistic communities, and ways of living do not exhaust the discussion of faith. However, Cobb adopts this community approach and says:

> According to this understanding, which is mine, to be a Christian is to locate oneself in the Christian community. This community is a changing one, growing out of a long history and moving into an uncertain future. Being a sociohistorical movement does not, of course, differentiate Christianity from other major traditions. What differentiates the Christian movement is its particular origin and history. It originated in events in Israel centering on Jesus and the community that grew up around him. Crucial for the development of this community was its interpretation of the nature and mission of Jesus after his death and his appearances to his followers. For simplicity, this complex of historical occurrences can be called "the Jesus-event."[17]

Cobb combines the claim that one should only be a Christian if one finds the community's claims compelling with the idea that all ideas are culturally shaped:

> This way of understanding Christianity recognizes that beliefs are culturally shaped and have their role and meaning within the community. They are not ultimate statements about absolute truth. Believers are not to be required to accept them if they do not commend themselves by their own persuasiveness and illuminating power.[18]

Of course, it could be true that one should only accept the claims of Christianity if one finds them compelling and that truth is not relative to a historical community. However, in one way, this is consistent with the American approach to religion as a sect among many others that must keep each other in check. This approach sidesteps the idea that some religious claims are true and, instead, thinks of them in terms of the power they wield in society.

It is difficult to decouple believing something is true from believing it is compelling. To believe something means to believe it is true. We only need to say "I believe it," not "I believe it is true," because this is assumed in believing. So is believing a community is compelling something more than believing it is true? It is likely that Cobb is importing noncognitive elements into considering what claims to accept. We may not know ourselves enough to know why we find some things compelling. If we knew our most basic beliefs, we would be able to start figuring out why one worldview is compelling another is not. We can see this in how he identifies the central teachings of Christianity.

CHRISTIANITY AND CHRIST

Cobb claims a Christ-centered approach to Christianity. "The central teaching of the Christian movement is about Jesus and 'Christ.' The question is how we are to understand the originating events of our movement and what they call on us to do today. Jesus is at the center of those events."[19] This is a common approach among those who do not accept the authority of scripture or general revelation. We have seen Emerson and Tillich also appeal to the person of Christ and yet abstract this from scripture and, instead, interpret in terms of their monism and pantheism. In Cobb's case, he relies on Whitehead's process theology:

> The Whiteheadian form of postmodernism offers another option. Christians can bring their understanding of God's presence in the world into relation with what we learn from historians who omit this. We can thereby come to fresh judgments as to how God was present in Jesus and in the early church. This enables us to take seriously the efforts of the church fathers to understand God's

> incarnation in Jesus even while realizing that some of the issues they raised and the conceptual categories available to them were different from ours. Whitehead makes this possible by providing a postmodern philosophical grounding for the widespread Christian belief that God is present and active everywhere. In a quite technical sense, God is immanent in all things. If so, God was immanent in Jesus and in the community that surrounded him and subsequently developed into the church. Given this starting point, the problem in formulating a Christology is quite opposite to that which confronted the church fathers. For them, thinking of creatures and God as externally related substances, the problem was how to affirm that, nevertheless, in this one unique case, God was internal to a human being. Since for them supernaturalism was no problem, they could do so easily by thinking of some portion of the human Jesus as replaced by the divine. But they resisted this option, because the assertion of the full humanness of Jesus was important to them. Accordingly, they developed the idea that one being could be commingled with another without loss of distinctness. In doing so they moved toward a doctrine of internal relations. They employed this doctrine also in understanding how the members of the Trinity mutually constituted one another.

Cobb argued that this thinking about the Trinity was an advancement over Greek philosophy because of how it understood the internal relations of the Trinity. He used Whitehead's thought to contextualize the Trinity in Process Theology.

> Whitehead believed that in their reflections on the Trinity and the incarnation, the Alexandrian and Antiochene theologians made a fundamental metaphysical advance over Plato by developing a doctrine of internal relations. Christians can now begin where the church fathers ended. Not only was God present in Jesus without reducing his humanity in any way but also God is present in all of us. Hence the literal affirmation of incarnation is unproblematic. But the doctrine of incarnation was not simply about God's presence in the world. It was also about the unique authority and nature of Jesus. It is this that now challenges us.[20]

Cobb raises questions about what exactly Christ has saved humans from. In what sense is Christ the Savior? He dismisses many of the common answers that have been prevalent in American history and the history of Christianity. These include that Christ saves humans from a future state of hell or an angry God or sin and guilt. In terms of the latter, Cobb says that a therapist will be of more help than Christ. The other answers have lost any persuasive effect, according to Cobb. Instead, Christ teaches us about the love of God and the forgiveness of God. The threat of punishment from an angry God seems remote and part of an antiquated idea of God. If this is all that salvation amounts to, then "salvation seems somewhat peripheral to more burning concerns."[21] In its place, Cobb suggests a transformation of the world:

> Jesus' expectation was of a transformed earth where God's purposes are realized. Those who thought it would come soon were disappointed. But understanding salvation in terms of the healing of the planet with all its human inhabitants remains a worthy definition. It directs our attention to the suffering of the present day and indicates the importance of working for the transformation of society and the renewal of the Earth.[22]

We might call this an allegorical approach to scripture and the teachings of Christ. This means that a different context from that of the authors is imposed on the text. Whether it is Cobb's process theology or his incorporation of Buddhism, these are not the context of the Bible. As such, the meaning he gives to the life of Christ or the text of the Bible is not that of the original context. Minimally, this context was theistic, affirming that only God is eternal and that God is the creator, in contrast to process theology or Buddhism.

THEISM OR BUDDHISM

Cobb is sensitive to avoid skepticism. In order to do this, he works to show that religious claims can be made to be complementary to each other. This is true for the Abrahamic faiths. He thinks these can be shown to complement rather than compete with each other. However, he also wants to show this can be done between the Abrahamic faiths and Buddhism. In order to do this, a new and what he calls radical view of God must be adopted.[23] The problem as he sees it is between a transcendent view of God in the Abrahamic faiths and an immanent

God in the Buddhist faith. In order to make these complementary, he adopts a view of transcendence that is acceptable to Buddhism.[24] However, what is interesting is that in making this change in the definition of God so that it is acceptable to Buddhism, he ends up with a definition of God that is not acceptable to theism. He recognizes some of the difficulties: "Most Christian thinkers who have sought to bring reconciliation between Christianity and Buddhism have not only desubstantialized God, but also largely identified God with Buddha-nature. This move makes sense for those who have previously identified God with Being Itself."[25]

Cobb believes that some forms of Buddhism are compatible with the theistic view of God:

> A still clearer teaching about what Christians can call God is to be found in the Lotus Sutra, one of the most influential of Buddhist scriptures. Here, in addition to the many Buddhas inhabiting the many worlds, there is one universal and everlasting Buddha. This Buddha is represented through or manifested in all the more particular Buddhas, such as Sakyamuni. Thus Sakyamuni is, at the deepest level, this universal Buddha. This universal Buddha is far removed from the impassibility and the omnipotence of the God of classical Christian theism. Buddha is above all compassionate, seeking the salvation of all, and often frustrated by human resistance. But the Sutra's analogy of the universal Buddha with a loving father certainly shows its resonance with the God of the Bible. It is fully compatible with the ideas proposed from the Christian side previously stated.[26]

However, this view of God does not include the theistic view of sin or the need for atonement. Cobb has already dismissed these as antiquated, so it is not a problem for his theology. The idea that Christ is one form of a Buddha is not acceptable to historic Christianity, nor is the idea that the prophets of Judaism and Islam are Buddhas acceptable to those religions. As is true in compromise positions, Cobb requires the theistic religions to accept the monistic view of Buddhism, which is not part of their historic teaching. The question remains: which side of the compromise is to be accepted? The historic teaching of Christianity found in Genesis is that God created one world and created that world very good (without evil). It assumes that sin is the rejection of what can be known about God and the good. In contrast to this, Cobb adopts a view that rejects certainty:

> This book adopts the opposite approach. It recognizes the impossibility of certainty but affirms the value of general theories as hypotheses with varying degrees of warrant. It regards the testing of such hypotheses as endless but fruitful. It operates on the hypothesis that the totality of the reality in which we are immersed is incomprehensibly complex. Within that complexity, it theorizes, many different patterns can be traced. The descriptions of these patterns often appear contradictory and mutually exclusive. As verbal formulations, indeed, they are likely to be just that. But more careful statement can often show that, however different the patterns are, the reality of one pattern does not necessarily deny the reality of patterns that other communities believe they have discerned.[27]

If there is nothing about which we can be certain, this includes the highest good and the knowledge of God. This means that nothing is clear. If nothing is clear, then this includes any distinction between good and evil, between humans and nonhumans, between God and not-God. The loss of all distinctions is called nihilism. Nihilism is the outcome of this form of postmodernism.

We see this in Cobb's analysis of what it means to be a human in contrast to a potential human:

> Destroying a potential human person, nevertheless, is a quite different matter from destroying a human person. In nature generally, most such potentials are not realized. Indeed, they could not be realized. Only a tiny percentage of potential oaks become oaks, for example. In human beings, only a tiny percentage of sperm fertilize ova. The idea that every potential for life, even human life, should be actualized is, of course, absurd. The decision to actualize potentials should always be made in the context of considering other potentials that may be thwarted in the process. But because of the great value of the actuality that is prevented by destroying the fertilized ovum, its destruction should never be casual. As the embryo develops, its intrinsic value increases. Nevertheless, it remains trivial in comparison with the value of what it has the potential to become.[28]

Cobb analyzes the value of a fetus in terms of its ability to feel pleasure and pain:

> The intrinsic value of the fetus becomes a significant concern only when the central nervous system develops to the point where there are unified experiences. Causing pain to the fetus after this time should be a matter of moral consideration. This consideration increases as the subjective life of the fetus grows. Even then, however, the intrinsic value of fetal experiences is analogous to that of animals to which we assign quite limited value on an individual basis. It is still the potential value that should dominate our moral reflections. The view presented here is opposed to treating any one principle as an absolute. Every decision about abortion must balance a variety of considerations. The values of the pregnant woman and of the fetus are especially important. As time passes, the balance shifts toward the fetus, but never to the point that the woman's life should be sacrificed to it.[29]

We can see from these considerations that matters of law are not separable from metaphysics and epistemology. It is a utilitarian method that Cobb uses to decide that in some instances abortion is acceptable because it increases the happiness of the mother while only ending the life of a fetus is grounded in his metaphysics. His reliance on personal experience and intuition led to his beliefs about what is real, which in turn formed his beliefs about what is good (in terms of pleasure and pain). This is the relationship we have seen throughout this book.

CONCLUSION

The question of the legality and morality of abortion remains a deeply divisive issue. The Supreme Court's decision is questioned by many. We saw that it is rooted in skepticism about what constitutes a human person before birth. This same skepticism led to utilitarian considerations about viability that would not factor into the discussion if the Court thought that it could be known that the unborn child is equal in humanity to those who have already been born.

Is it self-evident that all men have been created equal? We have traced the idea of self-evidence as it relates to what can be known through challenges about the nature of knowledge and the nature of God. Deep divisions remain. These divisions lend support to philosophical skepticism. However, they do not necessarily imply the truth of skepticism.

There are only so many basic beliefs that are used to interpret experience. And there are only so many ways that these basic beliefs are justified. We have considered reason as understood to mean naturalistic thinking, common sense, and intuition. In each case, we used reason as the laws of thought to critically analyze basic beliefs for meaning and consider the role of common sense and intuition. At this point in American history, there remains a need for agreement at the foundational level about what can be known, what is real, and what is good. Although the Declaration of Independence set out a formula for these, it has not proven to be successful in responding to the challenges since that time. A deeper foundation is needed. This is one that would use reason to show what can be known about God and the good.

CONCLUSION: BUILDING ON PAST INSIGHTS

A Philosophy of History

We began this study with the idea that the Declaration of Independence presents a kind of creed about foundational truths. It claims that some things are self-evident about God the creator and the human good. This covers the areas of epistemology, metaphysics, and ethics. We have also seen how these areas have come to play a part in court decisions and therefore the law. In the preceding chapters, we have seen how differences in epistemology lead to differences in metaphysics and from there to differences in ethics and the legal realm. Reliance on naturalism, intuition, and common sense did not help arrive at knowledge but only more divisions.

In the Introduction, we spoke about the principle of unity. It says:

> **If unity can be achieved about the most basic questions humans can ask, then unity can be achieved on less basic questions that presuppose what is basic.**

In the beginning of this book, we related the principle of unity to the principle of clarity. There must be something clear. We can clearly distinguish between God and non-God, between human and nonhuman, and between the good and what is nongood. Since these concepts are basic to all thought, we are obligated to know them. The failure to know is culpable ignorance. Unity can only be achieved when we can show what is clear.

We have seen various attempts at unity by appealing to common sense, intuition, or philosophical materialism (in the name of science). These have all failed to give knowledge at the basic level and have therefore not resulted in unity. We have also seen how skepticism and fideism are used to avoid the need for knowledge at the basic level. Pragmatism is a kind of skepticism. It says that what is true is what works. However, what works is relative to the desires of an individual or the goals toward which one is working. We cannot know what actually "works" without knowing what is actually good. Pragmatism is used to avoid the need for knowledge at the basic level while also not critically analyzing its own assumptions.

Unity requires knowledge of the basic questions about God and the good. If we can come to have knowledge about these, then we can have unity. While we do not have knowledge but only opinion, divisions will remain. Knowledge is not the same as opinions. Opinions can be true or false. Having a true opinion can be an accident. Having knowledge means one has a true belief and is able to demonstrate the truth of that belief. The questions before us remain the same as they have been throughout human history.

When we are asking about God, we are asking about what has existed from eternity, what is without beginning. We have seen that philosophical materialism says that matter, in some form, has existed from eternity and that matter is all that exists. We saw that Emerson taught a kind of pantheism in which consciousness is the highest reality and presumably has existed from eternity. The material world, in this form of idealism, is reduced to consciousness and has no reality in itself. These are two kinds of monism: material monism and spiritual monism. They stand in logical contradiction to the claim that only God is eternal and that God is the creator of all else. If we are to have unity, we must address the question of what is eternal: matter, consciousness, or God the Creator.

We have also seen that these competing views about what is eternal lead to competing views about the highest good for humans. In each case, knowledge of what is real is the highest good and produces a law relative to that good. However, material monism, spiritual monism, and God the Creator are each different and therefore give different highest goods and different outcomes for law. This is true for both the moral law and the civil law.

The challenges that have been raised by skepticism, fideism, material monism, and spiritual monism are directed at the claim that it is self-evident that God is the Creator. Consequently, it cannot be said that belief in God the creator is self-evident. Instead, these challenges must be addressed. Doing so requires the use of reason, as the laws of thought, to critically analyze claims about what is eternal. If something is eternal, it cannot go through unique change such as the final burnout of the material universe or the attainment of enlightenment through pure consciousness. This violates the laws of identity and noncontradiction in that what is eternal is eternal and is not changing. God the Creator alone is eternal, and the creation is finite and changing.

There is a personal side to how an epistemology is chosen. Different personalities rely on different epistemologies as their default. For some, this may be common sense, for others intuition, for others the deliverance of the senses. In each case, beliefs about what is real follow. However, all persons, regardless of their default epistemology, can use reason to critically examine their assumptions. This is the first application of philosophy. The love of wisdom requires self-examination. Before we can go on to ask about the beliefs of others or of society at large, we must begin with examining our own basic beliefs and testing them for meaning.

There is a need for common ground in any society. This common ground establishes the unity that allows the society to function and flourish. This common ground involves understanding reason, the basic beliefs or presuppositions behind a worldview, and the highest good. If there is no common ground, then there can be no basis for discussion and coming to agreement.

The consequences of not having unity are an increasing division of purpose that ultimately undermines the ability of a society to remain one and integrated. The loss of unity is grounded in failing to know what is basic. This failure, in turn, leads to a loss of meaning. As meaning is lost due to the failure to know, it will be sought in noncognitive sources such as pleasure.

There are dichotomies in American history between tradition and individual experience, deontology and utilitarianism, heaven and this-worldly goods, and freedom and license. Science and religion can be included in these. This is especially true when science means empiricism limited by philosophical materialism and religion based on intuition.

Much of the debate about religion and law has focused on religion as revealed religion. Religion has tended to be reduced to belief in the supernatural and a set of moral codes needed to get into heaven. However, the Declaration of Independence started with claims about natural religion. In doing this, it was attempting to affirm that some things can be known by all persons at all times about God and the good. Natural religion as such has played little role in legal or social conflicts about religion and the state.

However, before we can know if there is revealed religion, we need to know if there is a God who has given special revelation. This is a question for natural theology or natural religion. If there is common ground, it must begin in the realm of natural religion. Some of the most influential Supreme Court cases have been based on skeptical claims about what can be known from general revelation.

Philosophical materialism that is behind Darwinism is a claim about what is real. The pantheism of Emerson or Tillich is also a claim about what is real. These are basic beliefs that reject theism. Just like there are only so many ways that people seek to justify their beliefs, so too there are only so many basic beliefs. Indeed, there are only two: the one that says all is eternal and the other that says only some (God) is eternal. Both philosophical materialism and pantheism say that all is eternal, although they disagree about what it is.

The question about what is eternal is a foundational question. It is a question that must be answered if there is to be unity. The Declaration of Independence *declared* its answer. But this answer, whether it is deism or theism, has been challenged. These challenges must be considered and responded to if unity is to be attained.

Religious liberty exists within the state because, among other things, the authority of the state has limits. However, this does not keep individuals from coming to attain knowledge. The idea that there will always be factions and sects divided over religious matters is based on the idea that knowledge is not possible in this area. Although those who make this claim support the belief by appealing to the reality of factions and sects throughout history, there has also been progress in many areas where there was once disagreement.

Can we have agreement about what is real? This requires asking if we can have agreement about the most basic beliefs concerning what is real. Disagreements about what to teach in public schools, about Darwinism and Intelligent Design, or about abortion and what it means to be equal are disagreements about what is real. The argument occurs at less basic levels such as public education and abortion. But behind these are presuppositions about what is real that usually go unnoticed, that are neglected.

One way to avoid looking at these presuppositions is to assert that we cannot know. Skepticism results when faulty means to knowledge are used and are unsuccessful. Thus, appeals to tradition, common sense, intuition, science/empiricism, and even reason when it is only partly used end in the failure to know, and this is used to justify skepticism.

Another way of avoiding the critical examination of basic beliefs is by claiming that beliefs do not matter. This is a shift toward noncognitivism. It says that beliefs play a very small role in our lives. According to this view, beliefs only come into our consciousness when we are asked about them or deliberately reflect on them. Most of the time we are simply living our lives and beliefs play almost no role.

The protection of religious liberty need not be based on skepticism. It can be rooted in the limits on authority of the different institutions of human society and on the nature of belief formation and attainment of knowledge. It can take into account the reality that not all persons want to know what is basic about God and the good. In a way, the questions about knowledge, what is real, and what is good are like all other areas of knowledge. In another way, they are not, because they are presupposed by all other areas of knowledge. If we do not have knowledge at the basic level, then we do not have it at levels that presuppose this basic level.

Although it is not self-evident that God created humans, it is clear to reason. When we ask if God exists, we are asking what has existed from eternity. In forming beliefs about what is eternal, we are using reason to distinguish "eternal" from "noneternal." There is a clear distinction between the concepts "eternal" and "noneternal." To say that nothing is eternal or that all is eternal attributes the property *eternal* to what is not eternal. This is a violation of the law of identity and also of the law of noncontradiction.

The hope as we end is that there is new attention paid to natural religion and what is clear about God and the good. Instead of getting stuck in old discussions about tradition and experience or common sense and intuition, we can make progress in knowing what is clear to reason about God and the good. Some truths are clear, God created humans equal, and God established a natural moral law written on their hearts that directs them toward the highest good of knowing God. Unity about these foundational matters will provide the basis for unity in other areas of life.

NOTES

INTRODUCTION: THE FORMULA OF THE DECLARATION OF INDEPENDENCE

1 Johnny Cash with U2, "The Wanderer," *Zooropa*, 1993.
2 Surrendra Gangadean, *Philosophical Foundation: A Critical Analysis of Basic Beliefs* (Lanham, MD: University Press of America, 2008).
3 Ibid.
4 Afterword, Samuel Moyn p. 249, in Kate E. Tunstall, *Self-Evident Truths? Human Rights and the Enlightenment* (New York: Bloomsbury Academic, 2012).
5 Kate E. Tunstall, *Self-Evident Truths? Human Rights and the Enlightenment* (New York: Bloomsbury Academic, 2012), 111.
6 Frank Lambert, *Founding Fathers and the Place of Religion in America* (Princeton, NJ: Princeton University Press, 2006), 208.
7 Ibid., 209.
8 Ibid., 248.
9 Ibid., 206.
10 Ibid., 206.
11 Alvin Plantinga, *Warranted Christian Belief* (Oxford University Press, 2000), 114.
12 Ibid., 70.
13 Ibid., 70.
14 Ibid., 128.
15 Ibid., 68.
16 Ibid., 86.
17 Michael Bergmann, *Justification without Awareness: A Defense of Epistemic Externalism* (Oxford: Clarendon Press, 2006), 14.
18 Ibid., 16.
19 Ibid., 118.

20 Ibid., 207.
21 Ibid., 207.
22 Ibid., 208.
23 Ibid., 208.
24 Ibid., 215.
25 Ibid., 233.

1 THOMAS JEFFERSON AND THOMAS PAINE

1 Michael W. McConnell, "Establishment at the Founding," in *No Establishment of Religion: America's Original Contribution to Religious Liberty*, eds. T. Jeremy Gunn and John Witte (New York: Oxford University Press, 2012), 45.
2 Ibid., 49.
3 John T. Noonan Jr., and Edward McGlynn Gaffney Jr., *Religious Freedom: History, Cases, and Other Materials on the Interaction of Religion and Government* (New York: Foundation Press, 2011), 683.
4 Ibid., 534.
5 Ibid., 534.
6 Ibid., 534.
7 Ibid., 534.
8 Ibid., 535.
9 Ibid., 535.
10 Ibid., 535.
11 Ibid., 536.
12 Ibid., 535.
13 McConnell, *Establishment at the Founding*, 64.
14 Ibid., 65.
15 Ibid., 55.
16 Abraham Taylor, *The Insufficience of Natural Religion* (Boston: Drapper, 1755), 8.
17 Ibid., 15.
18 Ibid., 13.
19 Ibid., 6.
20 Ibid., 3.
21 Ibid., 3.
22 Thomas Jefferson, "A Bill for the Establishing Religious Freedom," http://www.religioustolerance.org/virg_bil.htm (accessed November 15, 2014).
23 Ibid.
24 Ibid.
25 Ibid.
26 Ibid.

27 Ibid.
28 Ibid.
29 Thomas Paine, *The Works of Thomas Paine* (2011), Kindle Edition ed., 6999–7001. Here and in other parts of the book I rely on the Kindle edition of widely available works. This is because I worked on this book while doing a great deal of commuting between Princeton and Arizona. It was not possible to keep all of my physical books with me, and digital books provided the solution.
30 Ibid., 7043.
31 Ibid., 7059.
32 Ibid., 7059.
33 Ibid., 7059.
34 Ibid., 7164.
35 Ibid., 7265.
36 Ibid., 7318.
37 Ibid., 7388.
38 Ibid., 7432.
39 Ibid., 7438.
40 Ibid., 7484.
41 Ibid., 7506.
42 Ibid., 7598.

2 THE REFORMED INFLUENCE ON COMMON SENSE PHILOSOPHY

1 Martin E. Marty, "Getting Beyond 'the Myth of Christian America,'" in *No Establishment of Religion*, eds. Jeremy Gunn and John Witte Jr. (Oxford: Oxford University Press, 2012), 367.
2 Ibid., 367.
3 John T. Noonan Jr., and Edward McGlynn Gaffney Jr., *Religious Freedom: History, Cases, and Other Materials on the Interaction of Religion and Government* (New York: Foundation Press, 2011), 538.
4 Ibid., 539.
5 Ibid., 539.
6 Ibid., 567.
7 "Constitution of Massachusetts," www.nhinet.org/ccs/docs/ma-1780.htm (accessed September 5, 2014).
8 Noonan and Gaffney, *Religious Freedom: History, Cases, and Other Materials on the Interaction of Religion and Government*, 547.
9 Ibid., 551.
10 Ibid., 566.

11 Alexander Hamilton, John Jay, and James Madison, *The Federalist Papers* (2011), Kindle Edition ed., 98.
12 Ibid., 98.
13 Ibid., 99.
14 Ibid., 9.
15 Ibid., 10.
16 Ibid., 31.
17 Ibid., 34.
18 Ibid., 34.
19 Ibid., 34.
20 Ibid., 35.
21 Ibid., 35.
22 Ibid., 35.
23 Ibid., 35.
24 Ibid., 35.
25 Ibid., 36.
26 Ibid., 168.
27 Ibid., 168.
28 Ibid., 169.
29 Ibid., 169.
30 Ibid., 170.

3 COMMON SENSE AND THE SELF-EVIDENT IN LAW

1 "Supreme Court Cases," http://supcourt.ntis.gov/ (accessed September 5, 2014).
2 Ibid.
3 Ibid.
4 Ibid.
5 Ibid.
6 Ibid.
7 Ibid.
8 Thomas Reid, *Selections from the Scottish Philosophy of Common Sense*, (Veritatis Splendor Publications, 2012), Kindle ed., 13.
9 Thomas Reid, *Thomas Reid's Inquiry and Essays* (Lexicos Publishing, 2012), Kindle ed., 15761.
10 Ibid., 15769.
11 Ibid., 5626.
12 Marion Ledwig, *Common Sense: Its History, Method, and Applicability* (New York: P. Lang, 2007).
13 William C. Davis, *Thomas Reid's Ethics: Moral Epistemology on Legal Foundations* (New York: Continuum, 2006), 6.

14 Ibid., 17.
15 Ibid., 20.
16 Reid, *Thomas Reid's Inquiry and Essays*, 5619.
17 Ibid., 14696.
18 Ibid., 14699.
19 Ibid., 14930.
20 Ibid., 14945.
21 Ibid., 14723.
22 Ibid., 14776.
23 Ibid., 14851.
24 Ibid., 25099.
25 Ibid., 25123.
26 Ibid., 25137.
27 Ibid., 25140.
28 Ibid., 25185.
29 Ibid., 25166.
30 Ibid., 25230.
31 Ibid., 5667.
32 Ibid., 5662.
33 Ibid., 5631.
34 Ibid., 5629.
35 Ibid., 14674.
36 Ibid., 15603.
37 Ibid., 15722.
38 Ibid., 15757.
39 Ibid., 15903.
40 Perry Miller, *American Thought: Civil War to World War I* (Holt, Rinehart, Winston, 1965), ix.
41 Ibid., ix.
42 Ibid., x.
43 Ibid., xi.

4 INTUITION AND THE SELF-EVIDENT IN LAW

1 John T. Noonan Jr., and Edward McGlynn Gaffney Jr., *Religious Freedom: History, Cases, and Other Materials on the Interaction of Religion and Government* (New York: Foundation Press, 2011), 662.
2 Ibid., 691.
3 Ralph Waldo Emerson, *Essays by Ralph Waldo Emerson* (The American Scholar, 2011), Kindle Edition, 12.
4 Ibid., 15.

5 Ibid., 98.
6 Newton Arvin, *Major Writers of America* (Harcourt Brace, 1962), 247.
7 Ibid., 250.
8 (Emerson, Harvard, American Religions, 173).
9 (Emerson, Harvard, American Religions, 175).
10 (Emerson, Harvard, American Religions, 177).
11 Ralph Waldo Emerson, "Divinity School Address," http://www.emersoncentral.com/divaddr.htm (accessed February 9, 2015).
12 Ibid.
13 Ibid.
14 Ralph Waldo Emerson, *The Transcendentalist* (2011), Kindle Edition, 129.
15 Ibid., 44.
16 Arvin, *Major Writers of America*, 246.
17 Ralph Waldo Emerson, *Nature* (2011), Kindle Edition, 5.
18 Ibid., 14.
19 Ibid., 25.
20 Arvin, *Major Writers of America*, 248.
21 Emerson, *Nature*.
22 Emerson, *The Transcendentalist*, 60.
23 Emerson, *Nature*, 12.
24 Ibid., 23.
25 Arvin, *Major Writers of America*, 247.
26 Ibid., 247.

5 NATURALISM, DARWINISM, THE SELF-EVIDENT, AND LAW

1 "Edwards v. Aquillard," http://www.law.cornell.edu/supremecourt/text/482/578 (accessed February 9, 2015).
2 Ibid.
3 Ibid.
4 Ibid.
5 Ibid.
6 Ibid.
7 Ibid.
8 Ibid.
9 Ibid.
10 Ibid.
11 Ibid.
12 Ibid.
13 Ibid.

14 Ibid.
15 Perry Miller, *American Thought: Civil War to World War I* (Holt, Rinehart, and Winston, 1965).
16 Ibid.
17 Ibid.
18 Ibid.
19 Charles Darwin, *On the Origin of Species by Means of Natural Selection, Or, the Preservation of Favoured Races in the Struggle for Life* (2011), Kindle Edition, 258.
20 Ibid., 259.
21 Ibid., 255.
22 Ibid., 256.
23 Cynthia Eagle Russett, *Darwin in America: The Intellectual Response, 1865–1912* (San Francisco: W. H. Freeman, 1976), 3.
24 David Berlinski, *The Devil's Delusion: Atheism and Its Scientific Pretensions* (New York: Basic Books, 2009), 179.
25 Ibid., 186.
26 Ibid., 187.
27 Ibid., 188.
28 Ibid., 189.
29 Ibid., 191.
30 Ibid., 86.
31 Ibid., 77.
32 Ibid., 39.
33 Susan Jacoby, *Freethinkers: A History of American Secularism* (New York: Metropolitan Books, 2004), 169.
34 Ibid., 6.
35 Ibid., 4.
36 Josiah Royce, "The Problem of Job," in *American Thought: Civil War to World War I*, ed. Perry Miller (New York: Holt, Rinehart, and Winston, 1962), 21.
37 Ibid., 21.
38 Ibid., 21.
39 Chauncey Wright, "Evolution of Self-Consciousness," in *American Thought: Civil War to World War I*, ed. Perry Miller (New York: Holt, Rinehart, and Winston, 1962), 31.
40 Ibid., 28.
41 Ibid., 31.
42 Ibid., 34.
43 Ibid., 37.
44 Ibid., 37.
45 Ibid., 38.
46 Ibid., 43.

47 John Dewey, "The Influence of Darwinism on Philosophy," in *American Thought: Civil War to World War I*, ed. Perry Miller (New York: Holt, Rinehart, and Winston, 1962), 222.
48 Ibid., 218.
49 Ibid., 220.

6 REVIVALISM, NEW RELIGIOUS MOVEMENTS, AND LAW

1 John T. Noonan Jr. and Edward McGlynn Gaffney Jr., *Religious Freedom: History, Cases, and Other Materials on the Interaction of Religion and Government* (New York: Foundation Press, 2011), 639.
2 Ibid., 641.
3 Ibid., 620.
4 Ibid., 622.
5 Ibid., 623.
6 Ibid., 623.
7 Charles Finney, *The Works of Charles Finney*, Kindle Edition ed., Vol. 1, 59588.
8 Michael S. Horton, "Charles Finney v. the Westminster Confession of Faith," http://www.mountainretreatorg.net/articles/charles_finney_vs_westminster_confession.shtml (accessed February 9, 2015).
9 Finney, *The Works of Charles Finney*, 59518.
10 Ibid., 59555.
11 Horton, *Charles Finney v. the Westminster Confession of Faith.*
12 Finney, *The Works of Charles Finney*, 72801.
13 Ibid., 61863.
14 Ibid., 72691.
15 Ibid., 72942.
16 Ibid., 72674.
17 Ibid., 72698.
18 Ibid., 72934.
19 Ibid., 72873.
20 Ibid., 72937.
21 Ibid., 72742.
22 Ibid., 72899.
23 Ibid., 72739.
24 Ibid., 67360.
25 Ibid., 72747.
26 Ibid., 72747.
27 Ibid., 59522.
28 Ibid., 59531.
29 Ibid., 59540.

30 Ibid., 59544.
31 Ibid., 64297.
32 Ibid., 65209.
33 Ibid., 64636.
34 Ibid., 64145.
35 Ibid., 63981.
36 Ibid., 59598.
37 Ibid., 63937.
38 Ibid., 63365.
39 Ibid., 63273.
40 Ibid., 63249.
41 Ibid., 61923.
42 Ibid., 59816.
43 Ibid., 59816.
44 Ibid., 59727.
45 Ibid., 4075.
46 Ibid., 7501.
47 Ibid., 8826.
48 Horton, *Charles Finney v. the Westminster Confession of Faith.*
49 Ibid.

7 LIBERAL THEOLOGY AND LEGAL TRANSFORMATIONS

1 "Supreme Court Cases," http://supcourt.ntis.gov/ (accessed September 5, 2014).
2 Ibid.
3 Ibid.
4 Ibid.
5 Ibid.
6 Louis Dembitz Brandeis, "The Opportunity of the Law," in *American Thought: Civil War to World War I*, ed. Perry Miller (New York: Holt, Rinehart and Winston, 1962), 332.
7 Ibid., 339.
8 Susan Jacoby, *Freethinkers: A History of American Secularism* (New York: Metropolitan Books, 2004), 44.
9 Paul Tillich, *Systematic Theology: Three Volumes in One* (New York: University of Chicago Press, 1967), 3.
10 Ibid., 6.
11 Ibid., 8.
12 Ibid., 9.
13 Ibid., 11.

14 Ibid., 11.
15 Ibid., 12.
16 Ibid., 12.
17 Ibid., 14.
18 Ibid., 15.
19 Ibid., 16.
20 Ibid., 16.
21 Ibid., 17.
22 Ibid., 19.
23 Ibid., 23.
24 Ibid., 26.
25 Ibid., 35.
26 Ibid., 38.
27 Ibid., 62.
28 Ibid., 83.
29 Ibid., 86.
30 Ibid., 94.
31 Ibid., 96.
32 Ibid., 105.
33 Ibid., 104.
34 Ibid., 120.
35 Ibid., 172.
36 Ibid., 82.
37 Ibid., 420.
38 Ibid., 422.
39 Ibid., 127.
40 Ibid., 129.
41 Ibid., 129.
42 Ibid., 163.
43 Ibid., 196.
44 Ibid., 47.
45 John 14:15.
46 Tillich, *Systematic Theology*, 272.

8 SECULAR AND RELIGIOUS GOODS IN THE TWENTIETH CENTURY

1 "Supreme Court Cases," http://supcourt.ntis.gov/ (accessed September 5, 2014).
2 Ibid.
3 Ibid.

4 Ibid.
5 Ibid.
6 Ibid.
7 Ibid.
8 Ibid.
9 Ibid.
10 Ibid.
11 John Cobb, *Postmodernism and Public Policy: Reframing Religion, Culture, Education, Sexuality, Class, Race, Politics, and the Economy* (Albany: State University of New York Press, 2001), xi.
12 Ibid., xiv.
13 Ibid., 7.
14 Ibid., 15.
15 Ibid., 15.
16 Ibid., 15.
17 Ibid., 16.
18 Ibid., 18.
19 Ibid., 19.
20 Ibid., 20.
21 Ibid., 21.
22 Ibid., 26.
23 Ibid., 48.
24 Ibid., 48.
25 Ibid., 48.
26 Ibid., 55.
27 Ibid., 172.
28 Ibid., 188.
29 Ibid., 188.

BIBLIOGRAPHY

Alley, Robert S. *The Constitution & Religion: Leading Supreme Court Cases on Church and State*. Amherst: Prometheus Books, 1999.

Anglim, Christopher. *Religion and Law in America: An Encyclopedic Dictionary*. Grey House Publishing, 2009.

Arvin, Newton. *Major Writers of America*. Harcourt Brace, 1962.

Barnett, S. J. *The Enlightenment and Religion: The Myths of Modernity*. New York: Manchester University Press, 2003.

Becker, Carl L. *The Declaration of Independence: A Study in the History of Political Ideas*. New York: Harcourt, Brace, 1922.

Bergmann, Michael. *Justification without Awareness: A Defense of Epistemic Externalism*. Oxford: Clarendon Press, 2006.

Berlinski, David. *The Devil's Delusion: Atheism and Its Scientific Pretensions*. New York: Basic Books, 2009.

Boyd, Julian P., and Gerard W. Gawalt. *The Declaration of Independence: The Evolution of the Text*. Hanover, NH: Library of Congress in association with the Thomas Jefferson Memorial Foundation, 1999.

Bradley, James E., and Dale K. Van Kley. *Religion and Politics in Enlightenment Europe*. Notre Dame, IN: University of Notre Dame Press, 2001.

Brandeis, Louis Dembitz. "The Opportunity of the Law." In *American Thought: Civil War to World War I*, edited by Perry Miller. New York: Holt, Rinehart, and Winston, 1962.

Burleigh, Michael. *Earthly Powers: Religion and Politics in Europe from the Enlightenment to the Great War*. London: HarperCollins, 2005.

Cobb, John. *Postmodernism and Public Policy: Reframing Religion, Culture, Education, Sexuality, Class, Race, Politics, and the Economy*. Albany: State University of New York Press, 2001.

Commager, Henry Steele. *Jefferson, Nationalism, and the Enlightenment.* New York: George Braziller, 1975.

Darwin, Charles. *On the Origin of Species by Means of Natural Selection, Or, the Preservation of Favoured Races in the Struggle for Life.* 2011. Kindle Edition.

Davis, William C. *Thomas Reid's Ethics: Moral Epistemology on Legal Foundations.* New York: Continuum, 2006.

Dewey, John. "The Influence of Darwinism on Philosophy." In *American Thought: Civil War to World War I,* edited by Perry Miller. New York: Holt, Rinehart, and Winston, 1962.

Edge, Peter W. *Religion and Law: An Introduction.* Burlington, VT: Ashgate, 2006.

Emerson, Ralph Waldo. *Essays by Ralph Waldo Emerson.* The American Scholar, 2011. Kindle Edition.

Emerson, Ralph Waldo. *Nature.* 2011. Kindle Edition.

Emerson, Ralph Waldo. *The Transcendentalist.* 2011. Kindle Edition.

Feldman, Stephen M. *Law and Religion: A Critical Anthology.* New York: New York University Press, 2000.

Finney, Charles. *The Works of Charles Finney.* Vol. 1. Kindle Edition.

Gaustad, Edwin S., and Mark A. Noll, eds. *A Documentary History of Religion in America.* 3rd ed. Grand Rapids, MI: W. B. Eerdmans Pub., 2003.

Gay, Peter. *The Enlightenment: A Comprehensive Anthology.* New York: Simon and Schuster, 1973.

Haakonssen, Knud. *Natural Law and Moral Philosophy: From Grotius to the Scottish Enlightenment.* Cambridge: Cambridge University Press, 1996.

Hall, Kermit L. *Conscience and Belief: The Supreme Court and Religion.* Vol. 8. New York: Garland Publishing, 2000.

Hamilton, Alexander, John Jay, and James Madison. *The Federalist Papers.* 2011. Kindle Edition.

Hammond, Phillip E., David W. Machacek, and Eric Michael Mazur. *Religion on Trial: How Supreme Court Trends Threaten Freedom of Conscience in America.* Oxford: AltaMira Press, 2004.

Hitchcock, James. *The Supreme Court and Religion in American Life.* Oxford: Princeton University Press, 2004.

Hitchcock, James *The Supreme Court and Religion in American Life, Vol. 1: The Odyssey of the Religion Clauses.* Princeton, NJ: Princeton University Press, 2008.

Hitchcock, James. *The Supreme Court and Religion in American Life, Vol. 2: From "Higher Law" to "Sectarian Scruples"*. Princeton, NJ: Princeton University Press, 2008.

Jacoby, Susan. *Freethinkers: A History of American Secularism*. New York: Metropolitan Books, 2004.

Jayne, Allen. *Jefferson's Declaration of Independence: Origins, Philosophy, and Theology*. Lexington: University Press of Kentucky, 1998.

Jefferson, Thomas. "A Bill for the Establishing Religious Freedom." http://www.religioustolerance.org/virg_bil.htm (accessed November 15, 2014).

Lambert, Frank. *Founding Fathers and the Place of Religion in America*. Princeton, NJ: Princeton University Press, 2006.

Latham, Earl. *The Declaration of Independence and the Constitution*. Lexington, MA: Heath, 1976.

Ledwig, Marion. *Common Sense: Its History, Method, and Applicability*. New York: P. Lang, 2007.

Maier, Pauline. *American Scripture: Making the Declaration of Independence*. New York: Knopf, 1997.

Malone, Dumas, Hirst Dillon Milhollen, and Milton Kaplan. *The Story of the Declaration of Independence*. New York: Oxford University Press, 1975.

Mannino, Edward F. *Shaping America: The Supreme Court and American Society*. Columbia: University of South Carolina Press, 2009.

Marty, Martin E. "Getting Beyond 'the Myth of Christian America.'" In *No Establishment of Religion*, edited by Jeremy Gunn and John Witte Jr. Oxford: Oxford University Press, 2012.

May, Henry Farnham. *The Enlightenment in America*. New York: Oxford University Press, 1976.

McCloskey, Robert G., and Sanford Levinson. *The American Supreme Court*. Chicago: University of Chicago Press, 2005.

Miller, Perry. *American Thought: Civil War to World War I*. Holt, Rinehart, Winston, 1965.

Miller, Perry. *The New England Mind: From Colony to Province*. Cambridge: Harvard University Press, 1953.

Miller, Perry. *The Transcendentalists, an Anthology*. Cambridge: Harvard University Press, 1950.

Morgan, Richard E. *The Supreme Court and Religion*. New York: Free Press, 1972.

Noll, Mark. *A History of Christianity in the United States and Canada.* Grand Rapids, MI: Eerdmans, 1992.

Noll, Mark A., ed. *Religion and American Politics: From the Colonial Period to the 1980s.* New York: Oxford University Press, 1990.

Nongbri, Brent. *Before Religion: A History of a Modern Concept.* New Haven, CT: Yale University Press, 2013.

Paine, Thomas. *The Works of Thomas Paine.* 2011. Kindle Edition.

Plantinga, Alvin. *Warranted Christian Belief.* Oxford University Press, 2000.

Prior, Charles W. A. and Glenn Burgess. *England's Wars of Religion, Revisited.* Farnham, England: Ashgate, 2011.

Regan, Richard J. *The American Constitution and Religion.* Washington, DC: The Catholic University of America Press, 2013.

Reid, Thomas. *Selections from the Scottish Philosophy of Common Sense.* Veritatis Splendor Publications, 2012. Kindle Edition.

Reid, Thomas. *Thomas Reid's Inquiry and Essays.* Lexicos Publishing, 2012. Kindle Edition.

Royce, Josiah. "The Problem of Job." In *American Thought: Civil War to World War I*, edited by Perry Miller. New York: Holt, Rinehart, and Winston, 1962.

Russett, Cynthia Eagle. *Darwin in America: The Intellectual Response, 1865–1912.* San Francisco: W. H. Freeman, 1976.

Sandberg, Russell. *Religion, Law and Society.* Cambridge: Cambridge University Press, 2014.

Smith, Steven D. *The Rise and Decline of American Religious Freedom.* Cambridge, MA: Harvard University Press, 2014.

Sweet, William Warren. "Natural Religion and Religious Liberty in America." *The Journal of Religion* 25, no. 1 (1945): 45–55.

Taylor, Abraham. *The Insufficience of Natural Religion.* Boston: Drapper, 1755.

Tillich, Paul. *Systematic Theology: Three Volumes in One.* New York: University of Chicago Press, 1967.

Tunstall, Kate E. *Self-Evident Truths?: Human Rights and the Enlightenment.* New York: Bloomsbury Academic, 2012.

Wilson, Jon. *The Declaration of Independence: Foundation for America.* Chanhassen, MN: Child's World, 1999.

Wright, Chauncey. "Evolution of Self-Consciousness." In *American Thought: Civil War to World War I*, edited by Perry Miller. New York: Holt, Rinehart, and Winston, 1962.

Zuckert, Michael P. *Natural Rights and the New Republicanism*. Princeton, NJ: Princeton University Press, 1994.

Zuckert, Michael P. *The Natural Rights Republic: Studies in the Foundation of the American Political Tradition*. Notre Dame, IN: University of Notre Dame Press, 1996.

INDEX

abortion, 157–60, 170
Age of Reason, The (Paine), 40
Amendment
  First, 31, 103, 125
  Fourteenth, 86, 158
  Ninth, 158
America, as a Christian nation, 50
animation, mediate, 157
anti-blasphemy laws, Massachusetts (1772) and Virginia (1792), 33
Apologetics, 144
Aquinas, Thomas, 144, 158
arguments (defined), 6
Aristotle, 3, 60
Arnauld, Antoine, 80
Assessment Bill (Virginia, 1785), 31
atonement, 55, 116
  Cobb and, 169
  Jefferson and, 40
  Paine and, 93
  Tillich and, 147
authority
  Constitutional source of, 8
  knowledge and, 2
  Mosaic, 43
awareness
  immediate, 91
  mystical a priori and, 145
  strong
    Bergmann and, 27
    defined, 27
axioms
  defined, 81
  logical, 81

Bacon, Francis, 104, 123
Baker v. Fales (1820), 53
Balanced Treatment Act (Arkansas), 103
Barnes v. First Parish in Falmouth (1810), 52
beauty, 97
beliefs
  basic, 11
    challenging, 5
    changes to, 5
    defined, 5
    interpretation of experience and, 104
    shared by comprting religions, 161
  competing, 65
  defined, 5
  foundational, 4
  ethics of, 9–10
  first principles and, 78
  individual, liberty of, 87
  religious, 69–70
    diversity and, 87
    testing, 7, 69
Bergmann, Michael, 26–29
Berkeley, George, 72, 81
Bhagavad-Gita, 90

Bible
  authority of, 128
  Cobb and, 168
  Jefferson, 40
  logos and, 149
  necessity for, 37
  Paine's rejection of, 40, 44
  reason and, 130
Bill for Establishing Religious Freedom, A (1777), 31, 41
Bill of Rights, 11
Brandeis, Louis, 104, 142
Brewer, David, 124
Buddha
  Christ as one form of, 169
  universal, 169
Buddhism
  causation and, 132
  Cobb and, 168–71
  idealism and, 89

Cantwell v. Connecticut (1940), 86
Carlyle, Thomas, 106
causality/causation, 132
  Hume and, 132
Christ, Jesus, 38, 57
  Cobb and, 166–68
  death of, 46
  Finney and, 129, 138
  as first created being, 87
  Jefferson and, 40
  as *logos*, 150
  as mediator, 55, 93
  as a metaphor, 150
  no creed but, 129
  Paine and, 44
  as Savior, 167
  Taylor and, 39
  Tillich and, 147
Christianity
  Cobb and, 163, 166–68
  as a cultural-linguistic system, 164
  Darwinism and, 110, 113
  heathen mythology and, 43
  historic
    Emerson and, 91–92
    tradition and, 92
  Tillich and, 153
church attendance, 32, 34
  Massachusetts law (1782) requiring, 34
  Paine and, 43
Church of England, 35
Cicero, 35
citizenry
  moral, 36
  virtuous, 17
clarity (defined), 9
Cobb, John, 161–71
cognitivism
  assumptions of, 76
  non-, 177
Coleridge, Samuel Taylor, 106
common ground, 18–21, 175
  defined, 18
  first principles and, 78
  Tillich and, 144–46
common sense, 28, 82–83
  authority and, 85
  first principles and, 75
  knowledge and, 82
  Philosophy, 72
    Darwin and, 105
    defined, 29
    empiricism and, 72
  Reid and, 73–75
community, 164–66
concepts
  beliefs and, 6
  concerning God, 102
  defined, 6
  reason and, 148
  theological, and the mystical a priori, 145
conscience, 50, 86
  freedom of, 18
consciousness
  Emerson and, 96–98
  ethics and, 96
  reality and, 99
  self-, 120

Constitution
  Declaration of Independence and, 7–8, 11
  factions and, 64
  God and, 8, 61
correlation, Tillich and, 149
covenant, 56, 105
  Tillich and, 147
creation
  ex nihilo, 103
  science
    defined, 102
    teaching, 102
Creationism Act, 102
creed
  Declaration of Independence as, 1, 15, 173
  defined, 4

Darwin, Charles, 57, 84
Darwinism, 100–4, 105–23, 176
  Dewey and, 122
  process theology and, 84
  theism and, 122
  true meaning of, 104
Declaration of Independence
  central claim of, 14
Declaration of Universal Human Rights (UN), 15
Deism
  decline in religious orthodoxy and, 38
  defined, 19
Dewey, John, 119, 121–22
diversity, 11
divisions
  within Christianity, 86
  defined, 11
  versus diversity, 11
  human, 66
  religious, 67
  secondary, 11
Douglas, William, 71
dualism (defined), 20

education, 51
  public, and neutrality, 100, 103
Edwards, Jonathan, 57, 90
Einstein, Albert, 114
Emerson, Ralph Waldo, 57, 88–98, 106, 113, 176
  Edwards and, 90
  Kant and, 94, 98
  Paine and, 93
empiricism
  British, 60, 72–73
  Paine and, 45
  proof and, 44
  radical, 132
  scepticism and, 84
Enlightenment, 14, 36, 60
  Christian scripture and, 61
  Emerson and, 95
  Scottish, 59
epistemology, 1–2
  defined, 1, 21, 74
eschatology
  defined, 63
  Social Darwinism and, 138
Establishment Clause, 101
  Creationism Act and, 102
  test of, 100
ethics
  of belief, 9–10
    Reid and, 79
  defined, 2
  Emerson and, 96
  human rights and, 21
  Tillich and, 154
Ethics of Belief After the Enlightenment, The (Anderson), 9
evangelism, Finney and, 135, 137
evidentialism
  argument for rejecting, 25
  defined, 25
evil
  God and, 26, 106
  good and, 3, 19, 63, 137
  moral, 105, 117
  natural, 63, 105, 163
    Darwin and, 107, 110
  necessity of, 118
  Royce and, 118

evolution, defined, 102
existence, struggle for, 122
experience
  authority and, 57
  categories of, 152
  existential character of religious, 146
  finitude and, 152
  knowledge and, 73
  noumenal world of being and, 94
  self-verification/-interpretation and, 57

factions, 11, 64–68, 143
  causes of, 66
  concerns of, 68
  controlling, 66
  defined, 64
faith, 164–66
Federalist Papers (Madison), 11
fideism
  defined, 19
  Finney and, 133
  Tillich and, 151
finitude (defined), 152
Finney, Charles, 56–57, 127–39
  Westminster Assembly and, 127
  Westminster Confession and, 127, 133
First Council (Jerusalem), 92
Foundation of Moral Obligation (Finney), 134
foundationalism, 61
  epistemology and, 77
free thinking (defined), 115–17
freedom, 12
  of conscience, 18
  inherent, to pursue the good, 12
  political, 12
    good and, 13
  religious, 16–18
    mid-twentieth century, 31
  tolerance and, 35–36
fundamentalism (defined), 143

Gangadean, Surrendra, 9–10
George, Robert, 104
God, 11–13
  belief in, 102
    experience and, 29
    first principles and, 79
    Paine and, 47
    Plantinga and, 80
    Reid and, 79
  concepts concerning, 102
  as Creator, 2, 10, 14, 24, 38, 89, 134, 174
    Emerson and, 93
    relation to humans as creations, 93
    religion and, 112
  Darwinist, 85, 105, 112
  defining, 2
  Deist, 19
  Dualist, 20
  Epicurean, 38
  as eternal, 152, 174
  Evidentialist, 25
  existence of, 26, 177
  Finney and, 131
  as a first cause, 47
  freethought and, 116
  as ground of being, 71, 152–53
  happiness and, 134, 136
  image of, 93
  as immanent, 167–68
  knowing, 3, 9–10, 152
  law and, 137
  logos as reasoning about, 146, 148
  man's relation to, the state and, 142
  Mythological, 44
  nature of, 20, 39, 55, 93, 97
    Emerson and, 88
    Jefferson and, 40
    Trinitarian and Unitarian, 87
  Paine and, 43
  Pantheist, 20, 85
  Pelagian, 133
  Puritan, 17
  religious theory and, 102
  revelation and, 150, 176
  Royce and, 118
  as transcendent, 168

as watchmaker, 116
Whitehead and, 162
Word of, 45, 47, 149
Goethe, Johann Woldgang von, 95
good
common, 50
highest (defined), 3
human, 11–13
Gould, Stephen Jay, 112
Graham, Billy, 58
Gray, Asa, 104
Great Awakening
First, 4, 16, 43, 57, 90
Old versus New Side in, 7, 57–58
Second, 127–39
Old versus New School in, 7, 58
Grotius, Hugo, 56, 60

happiness, 24, 52, 56, 115
Darwinian process and, 117
defined, 2, 117
Finney and, 135–36
individual, 57
lasting, 3
materialism and, 115
moral/natural law and, 136
private good and, 79
Hegel, Georg Wilhelm Friedrich, 84, 107
Heidegger, Martin, 152
Henry, Patrick, 31
heresy trails, 141
Hobbes, Thomas, 56, 60
Hodge, Charles, 110, 128, 134
Holmes, Jr., Oliver Wendell, 104, 119
Holy Trinity Church v. United States (1892), 124
Horton, Michael, 129, 138
Hume, David, 59, 61, 72–73, 81–83, 94, 121
Locke and, 94

idealism
American enthusiasm for, 104
Buddhism and, 89
transcendentalism and, 89, 94

imperative, categorical, 151
incarnation, 167
Jefferson and, 40
intent, criminal, 126
interest, conflict of, 65
intuition
beauty and, 97
defined, 91
Emerson and, 90–91, 95
reality and, 97

James, William, 104, 119
Jamestown, 17
Jefferson, Thomas, 1, 17, 31, 40–42, 116, 142
Jehovah's Witnesses, 86
Jesus-event, 165
judgment
defined, 6
Reid and, 75
justice
moral, 46
Paine and, 46
Justification Without Awareness (Bergmann), 27

Kant, Immanuel, 26, 84, 94, 151
Hume and, 94
Kierkegaard, Soren, 146
knowledge, 11–13, 174
authority and, 51
authority of supposed, 60
common sense and, 82
empiricist account of, 27
Enlightenment view of, 25
experience and, 73, 94
Emerson and, 95
first principles/primary truths and, 62
critiques of, 74
non-inferential, 28
opinions and, 59
postmodern contextualizing of, 163
Reid and, 59
relevation and, 151
responsibility and, 9
sociological approach to, 27

language, 118–20
  defined, 118, 120
law
  of excluded middle, 6, 22
  of identity, 6, 22, 175, 177
  of love, 155
  moral, 51
    defined, 134
    Emerson and, 96
    Finney and, 134
    natural, 20, 37, 55, 63
    Tillich and, 156
  of Nature and Nature's God, 20
  of non-contradiction, 6, 22, 133, 175, 177
  self-evident and, 14–15, 100–4
  of thought, 22, 74, 82
liberty
  religious, versus religious regulation, 18
Locke, John, 26, 56, 60, 72, 80, 83–84, 94
logos, 146–49
Lotus Sutra, 169

Madison, James, 17, 61–68, 116
majority/majorities, 11, 115
Malebranche, Nicolas, 80
Marshall, Chief Justice John, 51
Marty, Martin E., 50
materialism
  Greek, 85
  philosophical, 102–3, 173
    Darwinism and, 113, 176
    defined, 3, 89
    naturalism and, 104–23
McConnell, Michael, 31–32, 35–36
McCosh, James, 84
meaning, 5–7
  defined, 5
  truth and, 10
Meno (Socrates), 65
metaphysics
  Darwinian, 110
  defined, 2, 20–21
  first principles of, 82
Meyer v. Nebraska (1923), 86
Miller, Perry, 83
ministers, sanctioning, 52
monism
  defined, 153
  Emerson and, 97, 110
  material, 174
  spiritual, 174
  Tillich and, 153
Monroe, James, 51
Moody, Dwight, 58
morality
  Hume and, 73
Mormonism, 86
Moyn, 14

naturalism, 100–4
  Darwin and, 109
  defined, 85
  philosophic materialism and, 104–23
nature, state of, 56
New Birth, 16
New Testament, Jefferson's rewrite of, 40
Newton, Isaac, 60, 104
Nicomachean Ethics (Aristotle), 3
Nietzsche, Friedrich, 92
nihilism, 5
  defined, 170
  total (defined), 9
Northwest Ordinance (1789), 51

objectivity (defined), 27
obligation, 137
occasionalism, 132
opinions
  authority and, 51
  competing, 65
Origin of Species (Darwin), 84, 105
Over-Soul, 90

Paine, Thomas, 40, 43–48, 93
pantheism, 176
  defined, 3, 20, 174
  Emerson and, 88

Parker, Theodore, 106
People v. Ruggles (1811), 33
perception
elements of, 72
Representative, 72
personhood, 157–61
Philosophical Foundation. A Critical Analysis of Basic Beliefs (Gangadean), 9
philosophy
Christian, 148
dialectic, 110
first application of, 175
Plantinga, Alvin, 25, 27, 29, 74
Plato, 3
politics
Madison and, 64
science of, 64
polygamy, 125–27
Positivism (defined), 121
postmodernism, reconstructive, 162
Pragmatism, 174
principles
common, 81
first, 59, 77–84
and common sense, 77
as common sense, 73–75
Madison and, 62
mistaking, 80
Plantinga and, 74
Reid and, 73
self-refutation and, 77
Problem of Job, The (Royce), 117
proof
empiricism and, 44
Paine and, 44
universal, 44
Protestantism, 18, 38, 83

quickening, 157–59

rationalism, 106
reality
cognitive approach to, 147
consciousness and, 99
Emerson and, 90, 97–98
reason, 5–7, 37, 148
autonomous, 150
common sense and, 82
defined, 6, 136
Enlightenment view of, 63
Finney and, 130
intuition and, 82, 90
as the laws of thought, 6
ontological, 151
religion and, 6–7
special revelation and, 39
Tillich and, 150
reasoning
common principles and, 81
redemption, 39
Jefferson and, 40
Paine and, 46
Reformation, 36, 54–58
challenges to, in America, 55–58
Christian, 55
secular, 55
regress, kinds of, 27
Reid, Thomas, 27–30, 59, 72–85, 147
Hume and, 73
relativism, moral, 114
religion
American, 50
revolution of, 16
civil rights and, 41
defined, 6, 125
by US Supreme Court, 70
disestablishment and, 50
establishment of, 32–36
requirements for, 32
natural, 36–40, 176
political and theological rationales for, 36
revealed, 176
supplying defects in government, 53
wars of, 58–61
Republic, The (Plato), 3
revelation, 149–50
defined, 153
general, 93
defined, 7
Paine and, 48

revelation (*cont.*)
miracles and, 60
natural, 151
reason and, 149
special, 88, 176
reason and, 39
universal, 46
Revolution, American
dichotomies around, 4
interpretations of, 4
Rex v. Woolston (1729), 33
Reynolds v United States (1879), 125
Reynolds, George, 125
ridicule, emotion of, 28
rights
civil, religion and, 41
human, 15
ethics and, 21
natural, 42
Roe v. Wade (1973), 157
Rorty, Richard, 115
Royce, Josiah, 117–18

science, theory of, 119
Scottish Realism, 83, 106
common sense and, 83
scripture, Paine and, 43
selection, natural, 107, 122
self-attesting
defined, 2
self-evident and, 21–24
self-interest, 17
separation
church/state, 42
wall of, 125
Sidgwick, Henry, 121
skepticism
defined, 19, 59, 177
empiricism and, 95
first principles and, 80
Reid and, 76
Scottish Enlightenment and, 59
Socrates, 12, 65
soul, 157
speciation, 113
species, modification of, 108
descent with modification, 109
St. Augustine, 160
Structure of Evolutionary Theory, The (Gould), 112
Sunday, Billy, 58
Supreme Court (US), 31, 42, 51, 69–70, 86, 100, 140, 142, 157
survival, struggle for, 114
Systematic Theology (Finney), 128

Taylor, Abraham, 36–40
theism, 103
Cobb and, 168–71
theology
Christian, postmodernism and, 164
natural, 35–36, 82
object of, 146
process, 84, 162–63
Cobb and, 168
Reid and, 166
Whitehead and, 166
requirements of, 144
of synthesis, 161
systematic, and correlation, 149
theological circle, 145
theos, 146
thought process (defined), 85
Tillich, Paul, 57, 71, 143–56, 176
tolerance
freedom and, 35–36
religious, 32
tradition, 164–66
transcendentalism, 88
idealism and, 89
Trinity
Jefferson and, 40
Paine and, 44
truths
classes of (defined), 130
first, 132
foundational, 173
intuitive, 130
but not universal, 132–33
meaning and, 10
of reason, 131
self-evident, 73, 100–4, 130–32

characteristics of, 130
defined, 2
Finney and, 131
law and, 14–15
self-attesting and, 21–24
self-evident *Truths?* (Moyn), 14
taxonomy of, 132
universal, 130

United States v. Ballard (1944), 140
United States v. Seeger (1965), 69–70, 143
unity, 17
principle of, 173
clarity and, 13
defined, 13

Veblen, Thorstein, 104
voluntarism (defined), 129

Warfield, Benjamin, 128
warrant, 170
Bergmann and, 27
Plantinga and, 27
Westminster
Assembly, 54
Confession of Faith, 54–55, 61, 63, 75, 84
as a *paper pope*, 56, 129
Shorter and Larger Catechism, 54–55, 63
Whitefield, George, 90
Whitehead, Alfred North, 162, 166
Whitfield, George, 58
Wisconsin v. Yoder (1972), 32
Witherspoon, John, 72, 83
Wordsworth, William, 95
Wright, Chauncy, 118–21

Young, Brigham, 125

Lightning Source UK Ltd.
Milton Keynes UK
UKOW01n2335220915

259099UK00006B/89/P

9 781107 088184